A MAINLINE TURNAROUND

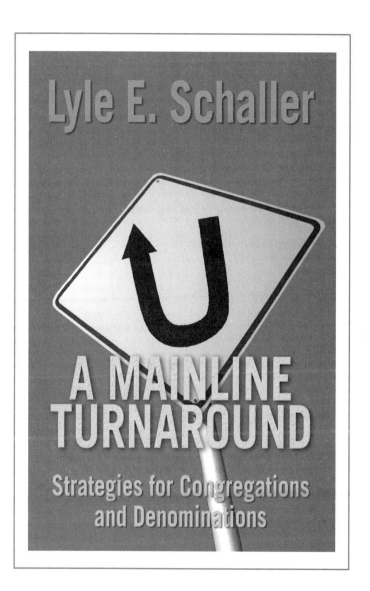

Lyle E. Schaller

A MAINLINE TURNAROUND

Strategies for Congregations and Denominations

ABINGDON PRESS
Nashville

A MAINLINE TURNAROUND
STRATEGIES FOR CONGREGATIONS AND DENOMINATIONS

Copyright © 2005 by Abingdon Press

All rights reserved.

Library of Congress Cataloging-in-Publication Data

Schaller, Lyle E.
    A mainline turnaround : strategies for congregations and denominations / Lyle E. Schaller.
      p. cm.
    Includes bibliographical references.
    ISBN 0-687-05401-X (alk. paper)
    1. Church renewal. I. Title.

    BV600.3.S34 2005
    262'.001'7—dc22

2004029950

05 06 07 08 09 10 11 12 13 14—10 9 8 7 6 5 4 3 2 1

MANUFACTURED IN THE UNITED STATES OF AMERICA

To Arlene Johnson

We are inspired by your commitment
to Jesus Christ
and grateful for your leadership,
your wonderful spirit,
and
your charming smile!

CONTENTS

INTRODUCTION 1

CHAPTER ONE: **WHAT HAPPENED?** 7
A Detour Through Recent History 8
Preparing for the Post–World War II Era 11
And Next Came the 1960s! 15
Where Do You Point Your Finger? 17
What Changed? 20
What's the Point? 37
What Have Been the Recent Outcomes? 39
The First Step 42
A Possible Second Step 42
That *Big* Step 45
Which Rule Book? 48

CHAPTER TWO: **WHICH RULE BOOK?** 51
What's the Difference? 52
The Rights of the Dissenter 58
From Vertical Systems to Horizontal Partnerships . . . 61
What Is the Central Organizing Principle? 64
Donor-driven or Recipient-driven? 66
Six Limitations 69
Why Chase This Rabbit? 74

CHAPTER THREE: **DESIGNING A TURNAROUND STRATEGY** . . . 81
What Is the Assignment? 82
What Are the Criteria? 87
Where Do Americans Go to Church? 88
The Criteria for Setting Priorities 89
    I. and II. The Top Two Components 91

III. Identify the Primary New Constituency 93
IV. Replace Factionalism and Intradenominational
    Quarreling with a Unifying Vision of One Clearly
    Defined Role for Your Denomination 97
V. The Staff Configuration 100
VI. The Fragile Nature of Very Large
    Congregations 101
VII. The Power of Peer Learning 106
VIII. From Geography to Affinity 108
IX. Where Will the Babies Born in 1985 Go to
    Church? 109
X. The Multisite Option 119
XI. Relocation 120
XII. Plant New Missions! 125
XIII. Trust and Empower the Laity! 127
XIV. Encourage Lay-led House Churches 129
XV. Integrate Our Anglo Congregations 131
XVI. Staffing Small Congregations 135
XVII. Utilize the Power of Television 139
XVIII. Revitalizing Those Aging and Numerically
    Shrinking Congregations 141
XIX. Staff the Position of Risk Management 144
XX. Encourage Congregational Mergers 145
XXI. Transform the Culture 146
How Do You Transform the Denominational
Culture? 149

CHAPTER FOUR: **THE MULTISITE OPTION** 153
Does This Belong on Your List? 156
Create the New 157
Adopt Those Who Want Help 160
Can We Have Our Cake and Eat It Too? 162
One Messenger or a Collegium? 165
Four Lines of Demarcation 168

CHAPTER FIVE: **PLANT NEW MISSIONS** 169
The Historical Context 170

The Changing Context 173
The Fourth Great Awakening 180
Who Initiates? 183
Twenty-one Questions 186
  1. Who Is in Charge? 186
  2. What Is the Vacuum? 188
  3. Is Leadership the Key? 191
  4. How Do You Define the Primary Constituency? 193
  5. What Stage of the Faith Journey? 195
  6. What Is Your Theological Position? 196
  7. What Will Be the Central Identity? 198
  8. How Competitive? 200
  9. Do You Affirm Territorial Monopolies? 200
  10. A Great Good Place? 201
  11. What Else Is on the Agenda? 204
  12. What About the Minister's Fan Club? 205
  13. Which Immigrants? 206
  14. Who Are the Most Neglected? 207
  15. Which Strategy Do You Prefer? 209
  16. Where Can We Cut Costs? 211
  17. Where Do We Begin? 213
  18. How Many? 214
  19. What Do You Count? 216
  20. Soloists or Teams? 218
  21. What Is the Road to Success? 218

CHAPTER SIX: **HOW DO WE PAY FOR IT?** 221
Five Different Appeals 223
What Is Counterproductive Behavior? 225
What Could Be the Most Productive Approach? . . . 227

CHAPTER SEVEN: **THE BIG QUESTION** 231
Three Basic Generalizations 232
Four Questions 233
Another Perspective 234

NOTES 239

INTRODUCTION

Ninety-nine years ago a combined total of thirty-six denominations accounted for approximately 128,000 or two-thirds of all the 195,000 Protestant congregations in the United States. Those three dozen denominations also included nearly 12 million members or nearly three out of five of the 21 million members of those 195,000 Protestant congregations in America in 1906.

During the next one hundred years the population of the United States increased 3.4 times from 85 million in 1906 to 289 million in 2005. What happened to those thirty-six denominations? First, thanks to a series of mergers and reunions those thirty-six have been transformed into ten.[1] Second, if the number of congregations and members had increased at the same rate as the increase in population, these ten denominations would have included at least 440,000 congregations in 2005. The actual number in 2005 was approximately 86,000, a decrease of 42,000 from 1906.

Those ten Protestant denominations also would have claimed a combined total of at least 39 million confirmed members in 2005 if their numerical growth had paralleled the increase in the American population. The actual number in 2005 was approximately 22 million confirmed members.

The obvious and indisputable number one explanation for the decrease in the size of those current numbers is death. Approximately 100 percent of those 12 million members of 1906 have died. A second obvious explanation can be summarized in the word "competition." During those same ninety-nine years, the Southern Baptist Convention nearly doubled the number of affiliated congregations and increased

1

its membership sevenfold. If their numbers are combined, the nondenominational congregations have a larger presence in American Protestantism than is represented by the Southern Baptists. The Assemblies of God traces its origins back only to 1914, but by 2005 included 13,000 congregations with a combined average weekly worship attendance of 1.7 million, one-half the average for the much larger United Methodist Church. That rising tide in the number of residents of America during the twentieth century did not lift all the ships in that religious harbor equally!

Will history repeat itself during the next ninety-nine years? Some of the Protestant denominations certainly will increase their numbers while others will experience a decrease. Which will grow? Which will decline in numbers?

This observer's answer is those mainline Protestant denominations in the United States that are both able and willing to design, adopt, and implement a turnaround strategy should be able to double or triple the size of their constituency by the end of the twenty-first century. The two key words in that optimistic statement are "able" and "willing." For a variety of reasons, including ideology, the power of tradition, and/or a dysfunctional organizational structure, some of these mainline denominations will not be able to reverse their numerical decline. That resulting vacuum has been, is, and will be filled by new movements, associations, denominations, and that rapidly growing number of large independent or nondenominational congregations.

The first chapter is devoted to that theme. The Twin Trade Towers were designed to collapse if the unexpected occurred. Several of the mainline Protestant denominations were redesigned in the years after World War II to reach and attract the generations born in the 1890–1930 era. As the decades rolled by, four changes made that design vulnerable to failure. American culture of the 1950s was replaced by a new and different culture. Second, the generations of Americans born after 1960 turned out to be unlike their parents and grandparents. Third, those new waves of immigration from Latin America and the Pacific Rim countries did not resemble the earlier waves of immigrants from Western Europe.

The fourth change was the entire economy became far more competitive. The rising level of competition that really began in the 1940s has transformed the economic model for agriculture, mining, transportation, higher education, the delivery of health care services, entertainment, recreation, retail trade, manufacturing, financial services, and nearly every other facet of American life. The competition among the churches today for future constituents is far greater than it was in the 1950s! One consequence is the "business plan" or the "ministry plan" for denominations that worked in the 1950s has become either obsolete or counterproductive. That is the theme of the first chapter.

Another change is the shift in the American culture from vertical organizational systems to horizontal partnerships. One consequence is the ministry plan that worked so well in a religious system organized as a high expectation, high commitment Christian body based on clearly defined and widely supported legal principles requires a different rule book for all the players than the system in which most of the players act on the assumption that this is a voluntary association. That is the theme of the second chapter.

The heart of this book is the focus on designing a customized turnaround strategy for your denomination. Twenty-one possible components of that strategy are described and evaluated in a long third chapter.

Two of those components, however, are so complex, so controversial, and so important they each deserve a separate chapter. Thus the fourth chapter discusses the multisite option while the fifth chapter raises a series of questions, the answers to which will influence the design of your church-planting strategy.

A brief sixth chapter suggests alternative approaches to financing the implementation of your denominational turnaround strategy. The last chapter raises a widely neglected issue. What should you do with your own people, and what should you outsource to specialists?

If you want to reduce the contents of this book to three themes, here is that summary.

The first theme traces back to Sir Isaac Newton's first law of motion published in 1687. It states a body in motion will continue in motion in the same direction unless acted on by outside forces. The translation of that to mainline American Protestantism in the post–World War II era is that those denominations experiencing numerical growth in the 1950s would have continued to grow unless acted on by outside forces. Those forces that have reversed that direction of growth include: changes in the American economy; the arrival of new generations who did not carry the same value system as their parents; the fourth great religious revival that began in the 1960s and produced more competition; waves of new immigrants from the Pacific Rim and Latin America; the suburbanization of the American population; denominational mergers; litigation; the increased costs of compensation and retirement benefits for the clergy; the sharp increases in the cost of land; the rising competition for people's discretionary time; an unprecedented wave of egalitarianism; and diversionary issues on denominational agendas that have encouraged a new wave of intradenominational quarreling.

The second theme is that the way to reverse years of numerical decline is to introduce a counterforce described here as a turnaround strategy that is *customized* to fit the polity, culture, and resources of your denomination.

The third theme is that the support for implementation of this customized turnaround strategy must exceed the combined support for all those forces that have been propelling your denomination on a downward curve.

How useful will the contents of this book be to the policymakers in your denomination? That answer will depend on the support that can be mobilized to design, adopt, and implement a turnaround strategy. That is a leadership issue covering at least five stages of a transition. The first stage requires leaders who can persuade their constituents that "we have a problem that must be addressed now!" That could be part of the state of the Church message delivered every January. It could be the central theme of the keynote address at the annual denominational meeting. Or it could be the introduction to that annual audit of performance described in the latter part of the first chapter.

The second stage calls for casting a compelling vision of what tomorrow could bring. The third stage consists of creating a customized ministry plan and *strategy* that is designed to transform that vision into reality. That is the focus of this book. The fourth stage demands leaders who can earn the support required to mobilize the resources required for implementation. A fifth and overlapping stage calls for the leadership needed during that implementation process. That is not a small assignment!

CHAPTER ONE

WHAT HAPPENED?

In the summer of 1980 a new 750-room hotel opened in Kansas City, Missouri. The Hyatt Regency was distinguished by a huge atrium covered by a steel and glass roof fifty feet above the floor. Three walkways at the second- , third- , and fourth-floor levels crossed the atrium and were suspended from the roof. The upper one on the west side connecting the fourth floors hung directly above the one connecting the second floors.

On a Friday evening in mid-July 1981, a dance was scheduled for the atrium with more than sixteen hundred people in attendance. Spectators on those second- and fourth-floor walkways began to stomp in rhythm with the music. The lower walkway was suspended from the one above it, so the two fell together, crashing down on the dancers and spectators below. A total of 114 people were killed, and another 200 were injured.

Eventually the National Bureau of Standards concluded the walkways were not designed to carry the stress created by that combination of the weight of the spectators plus the vibrations generated by the stomping.[1] In effect, the walkways were designed to fail if the unexpected happened.

Why did the Twin Towers at the World Trade Center in New York City collapse on September 11, 2001? The National Institute of Standards and Technology subsequently

7

concluded the combination of the intense heat, the inadequate fireproofing, the design of the floor trusses, the grade of the steel used in the construction, and other variables in the design meant that the buildings could crumble if the unexpected should happen. The unexpected came on a sunny September morning when the fuel-laden wings of two commercial aircraft traveling at nearly 600 miles per hour cut through those exterior walls and the fuel was ignited.

While it was completely unintentional, those walkways in that hotel in Kansas City and those office buildings in New York were designed to fail if the unexpected became the new reality. We see similar patterns in other areas of contemporary American life. New retail stores open with a business plan designed to fail. Many public schools are designed to produce failure among a significant number of students. Scores of new missions are planted every year using a design to produce failure. All across our society are hundreds of systems designed to respond safely and effectively to unanticipated circumstances while others are designed to fail.

A Detour Through Recent History

The half century following the Civil War brought a rapid increase in the number of Christian congregations and the number of church members in America. The combination of the frontier moving west, the immigration from Western Europe, the urbanization of America, the emancipation of the slaves, and the third great religious revival stimulated the demand for more churches. That demand increased the supply, and the increase on the supply side produced an increase in the demand. One of the consequences was the creation of several new denominations. Another was that growth curve in several denominations turned into a plateau in the late 1920s and early 1930s.

While the population of the United States increased by approximately 18 percent between 1926 and 1936, the census of religious bodies conducted by the United States Bureau of the Census in 1890, 1906, 1916, 1926, and 1936 reported an increase of only 2.3 percent in church membership between 1926 and 1936. Several religious traditions reported substantial increases, but several of what later were described as the mainline Protestant denominations reported decreases. The Mormons (LDS), for example, reported a 25 percent increase in numbers. The Roman Catholic Church reported an increase of 7 percent. Jews reported an increase of nearly 14 percent, the relatively new Assemblies of God reported an increase of 209 percent, while the Church of the Nazarene reported an increase of 114 percent, but the recently merged Evangelical and Reformed Church reported an increase of 7 percent, and Northern Baptists reported an increase of only 3 percent between 1926 and 1936.

On the other side of that ledger, the Southern Baptist Convention reported a decrease of 23 percent, the recently merged Congregational and Christian Churches reported a decrease of nearly 2 percent, and the Disciples of Christ reported a drop of 13 percent, while Presbyterians as a group reported nearly a 5 percent decrease in membership. The Methodist Episcopal Church, which had enjoyed an increase in membership of 25 percent between 1906 and 1916 and another increase of 10 percent between 1916 and 1926, reported a decrease of 14 percent between 1926 and 1936. The Methodist Episcopal Church South, which had experienced an increase in membership of 29 percent between 1906 and 1916, plus another gain of nearly 18 percent between 1916 and 1926, reported a drop of 17 percent between 1926 and 1936.

The Protestant Episcopal Church, which reported a net increase in membership of 23 percent and nearly 26 percent in the two previous ten-year periods, reported a drop of 6.7 percent for 1926–1936. Northern Presbyterians went from an increase of 36 percent in 1906 to 1916 and 16 percent in 1916 to 1926, to a decrease of 5.1 percent between 1926 and 1936. The southern Presbyterians reported an increase of 34 percent for 1906 to 1916 and 26 percent for 1916 to 1926, but experienced a modest drop of 0.4 percent for 1916–1926.

The fifty-year-old policy-makers in those mainline Protestant denominations of the 1950s, however, were more likely to be influenced by what had happened recently, rather than what had occurred back when they were in college. The statistical record in recent years was favorable. Thousands of new missions were being planted every year during the 1950s by Baptists, Presbyterians, Methodists, Lutherans, Episcopalians, and others. When three Methodist denominations were reunited in 1939 to form The Methodist Church, their combined membership was well under 6 million. Thirteen years later that total had grown to 9.2 million and by 1959 it was nearly 10 million.

While the Evangelical and Reformed Church had experienced a decrease in the number of congregations from 3,135 in 1916 to 2,875 in 1936 to 2,700 in 1956, the membership decline had been reversed and stood at 785,000 in 1956. The Congregational Christian Church reported 5,300 congregations in 1936, down from 7,163 in 1916, but by 1953 that number had grown to 5,573, and the membership had increased from slightly over 1 million in 1926 to 1.3 million.

The Disciples of Christ had recovered from a drop in membership of nearly 200,000 between 1926 and 1936. In 1953 they reported 1,848,000 members in 7,864 congregations compared to 1.2 million members in 5,566 congregations seventeen years earlier. The Southern Baptists had grown from 2.9 million members in 13,815 congregations in 1936, down from 3.5 million in 23,374 congregations ten years earlier, to nearly 7.9 million members in 29,481 congregations in 1953. The Northern Baptists had grown from 1.3 million members in 6,284 congregations in 1936 (down from 9,282 in 1906) to nearly 1.6 million members in 6,531 congregations in 1952.

The focus had changed. Those new congregations organized in the 1870–1915 era had been designed to serve people born before the transformation of American agriculture and prior to the drop in the immigration from Western Europe or the increase in the number of people who had not been born into slavery. They had been designed to serve adults who had not learned as teenagers to drive a gasoline-powered motor vehicle. Most of the Protestant churches founded in that 1870–1915 era were not designed to respond effectively to the rural-to-urban migration that marked the twentieth century.

By the mid-1920s it had become apparent that most of those aging congregations had a half dozen choices, (1) initiate and implement the changes required to reach and serve new generations, (2) watch their numbers grow smaller and focus their resources on institutional survival, (3) dissolve, (4) merge with another congregation in hopes of avoiding change, (5) focus on transmitting the Christian faith to their children, or (6) relocate the meeting place as part of a larger strategy to begin to outline a new role in their history. Most chose one of the middle four options on that list.

Preparing for the Post–World War II Era

After World War II a growing number of denominational policy-makers concluded it would be easier to organize new congregations to reach Americans born after 1920 than to reform the congregations founded in the 1880s to serve people born after the Civil War. It would be easier to organize new congregations to reach recent immigrants from the Pacific Rim than to transform congregations that had been organized decades earlier to reach and serve immigrants from Western Europe.

While thousands of American Protestant congregations founded before 1915 did implement the changes required to reach, attract, serve, nurture, assimilate, and challenge younger generations, tens of thousands were not able to make that transition. Likewise, while thousands of those new missions planted in the 1945–1960 era are now reaching the generations born after 1960, a larger number have either disappeared or are watching their constituents grow older in age and fewer in numbers.

Concurrently, denominational systems were being redesigned to be compatible with the culture, the economy, the American religious scene, and the social and demographic patterns of the 1950s. In several cases they also were designed to take better care of the clergy, to advance ecumenism, to facilitate denominational mergers, to enable denominational leaders to accept and fulfill a prophetic role, to challenge congregations to send money to denominational headquarters to hire people who would do ministry on behalf of congregations, to expand the capability of congregations to teach people of all ages the essential tenets of the Christian faith, and to resource that ministry often referred to as Christian education, to equip full-time professionals for that vocation as a Director of Christian education, to expand what was widely believed to be a needed regulatory role for denominational agencies, to require a seminary degree for ordination, to enhance denominational loyalty among the parishioners, to take advantage of the economy of scale by creating larger institutions, and to encourage interdenominational cooperation.

One reason this was done and one reason it worked was the 1933–1960 era was marked by a strong affirmation of the need for regulatory bodies in all segments of the American economy from public schools to commercial air travel to the practice of medicine to the sale of stocks and bonds to the use of airways for communication to the adoption of land use regulations.

A second reason it worked was the post-1941 era in American history marked a new peak in institutional loyalty. Patriotism was one expression of this. Loyalty to one's labor union or to one's alma mater or to one's employer or one's religious heritage or to one's lodge or service club or to the local public school or to a particular brand name were other expressions of institutional loyalty. As recently as 1955 only a tiny proportion of the Christian congregations in America were not affiliated with a clearly defined religious heritage. That heritage often was reflected in the name of the congregation. The concept of an independent Protestant church was seen as an oxymoron.

A third, overlapping reason was the competition for future constituents was far less intense than it is today. Inherited denominational loyalties encouraged churchgoers born before 1930 to look for a new church home affiliated with their denomination when they changed their address.

In 1956, for example, Methodist congregations in America received a combined total of 310,00 new members by letter of transfer from other Methodist churches. In 2002 the number of intradenominational transfers in The United Methodist Church had dropped to 109,000! In several denominations that earlier loyalty had been reinforced by ancestry, language, or skin color. Equally significant, the churchgoers of 1955 brought relatively low expectations as to what a church should offer parishioners. The adult churchgoers had been reared in a culture that taught, "This world offers you two choices—take it or leave it."

A fourth reason it worked was that respect for persons in positions of authority probably peaked in the 1930–1960 era. Respect for the value of academic credentials also peaked during the 1950s. That was *not* an egalitarian culture in 1955!

One consequence was the vertical top-down organizational structures of the Roman Catholic Church in America, the Protestant Episcopal Church, the various Methodist Episcopal denominations, and several other denominational systems were consistent with the culture.

Overlapping that, a fifth reason most of the denominational systems of the 1950s worked so well traces back to the first quarter of the twentieth century, but was reinforced by

the Great Depression. Who should determine the final destination of the charitable dollar?[2] For the wealthy the usual
answer was "the donor." For many Christians, however, the
right answer was "the people who have an overall view of
the larger picture and that are in a position to evaluate the
competing demands for money." That conviction reinforced
the concept that the basic needs of a congregation were a
meeting place, a name, a budget that included sending money
to denominational headquarters, volunteer leaders and
workers, and a pastor.

A sixth reason it worked is one that should not be discussed in ecumenical gatherings today. It goes back to one of
the oldest organizing principles in human history. How can
we transform a collection of strangers who tend not to
socialize with one another into a closely knit and cohesive
group? The answer is to identify a common enemy and rally
the people together in opposition to that common enemy.
That central organizing principle has been widely used to
amend the United States Constitution to prohibit the pro-
duction and sale of beverage alcohol, to create labor unions,
to mobilize people in war time, such as after December 7,
1941, to create the Civil Rights Movement in the 1950s, in
community organization efforts of the 1960s[3] in community
renewal efforts, and, most recently, following the fall of
Saddam Hussein in Iraq in 2003.

Between 1920 and 1960 the identification of the Roman
Catholic Church as the common enemy was a powerful unifying force in several of the larger American Protestant
denominations.

A seventh reason the denominational systems of the 1950s
worked so well was the differences among the various religious bodies in America on doctrine, polity, traditions, ancestry, social class, skin-color heritage, practices, and priorities
usually were greater than the differences among either the
clergy or the differences among the affiliated congregations.

While far from an exhaustive list, those were seven of the
reasons the denominational systems of America worked so

14

well. They were designed to be effective, relevant, influential, valuable, needed, and respected components of the larger religious scene in the America of the 1950s. They were designed to work in that context. They were not designed to fail.

And Next Came the 1960s!

The Twin Trade Towers in Manhattan were designed to withstand the impact of a medium-sized aircraft carrying only a modest load of fuel and traveling at a speed of perhaps 350 miles per hour.

September 11, 2001 brought an unanticipated change in events. A larger commercial aircraft carrying a full load of fuel and traveling at a speed close to 600 miles per hour crashed into one tower. A little later another aircraft carrying a full load of fuel crashed into the other tower. The design did not envision those events. Both towers were designed, unintentionally of course, to collapse if the unanticipated occurred.

The parallel is the denominational systems of 1955 were designed by and for adults born in the pre-1935 era to serve in the circumstances that marked the 1950s. They were designed to succeed. They were not designed to fail as long as the circumstances of 1955 continued to prevail.

Why are those systems far less relevant and effective today than they were in 1955? One reason is the people who designed them are no longer in charge.

A more important reason is most of the people they were designed to serve are now in retirement centers, nursing homes, and cemeteries. If the Second Coming of Christ had occurred in 1960, this would not be an issue. That delay, however, has created problems.

The 1950s brought two sets of radical changes that have undermined the assumptions on which those denominational systems of the 1950s were based.

The easiest one to document and explain divides into three categories called deaths, births, and immigration. Between 1960 and 2005 approximately 95 million Americans died, most of whom had been born before 1960. During those same forty-six years approximately 180 million babies were born in the United States. If we add in the babies born in the 1950s as part of that new constituency, the total is over 200 million new American-born constituents. In addition, 30 million immigrants came to America during these 46 years since January 1, 1960.

Those 200 million babies have been reared in a different cultural environment than were the denominational policymakers of 1955. The nine-year-old who had mastered all the skills required to use a computer or a cell phone, was watching his grandmother type the address on an envelope with an electric typewriter. "Hey, Dad! Come here!" called the grandson. "Grandma's got a keyboard with a built-in printer!"

Most of the babies born in the 1950s and later have been reared in a culture in which the projected visual images on motion picture, television, and computer screens are watched more hours per day than are the words printed in black ink on white paper. The preachers of 1955 were expected to excel as wordsmiths. The demand today is for ministers who excel as "imagesmiths."[4] Those babies born after 1950, and especially those born after 1965, have been reared in a culture in which messages come wrapped in entertainment.

The younger ones also have been reared in an environment in which the reliable, privately owned motor vehicle, cheap gasoline, the interstate highway system, low-priced commercial air travel, the Internet, and the cell phone have reduced the influence of geographical distance. One of the most significant statistics is the change in number of licensed motor vehicles. Between 1950 and 2005 the population of the United States nearly doubled. The number of privately owned automobiles, vans, and pickups has more than tripled. The ratio of cars to population has changed from two cars to seven people to close to two residents for every four motor vehicles. Today the word "walk" is used more frequently to describe how a baseball batter reaches first base than to describe how a parishioner travels to church.

In other words, the clientele those denominational systems of 1955 were designed to serve are well along in the process of being replaced by a new clientele. American context for "doing church in the twenty-first century" bears only a modest resemblance to the context of 1955.

Before resuming this historical detour, however, we need to take a quick look at a central theme.

Where Do You Point Your Finger?

When the actual outcomes do not match the desired results, whom do we blame? The natural tendency is to personalize disappointments. Someone failed to fulfill their responsibilities. Baseball fans agree America needs more highly skilled center fielders who also can hit forty home runs year after year as well as more shortstops who combine superb defensive skills with a high batting average and the ability to steal fifty bases every season. Similarly there is widespread agreement in America on the need for a larger number of parish pastors who combine the gifts of a loving shepherd, an inspiring preacher, a visionary leader, and an exceptionally productive worker.

An even greater shortage is in the number of denominational leaders who can revitalize dying congregations, raise a surplus of money, attract exceptionally competent parish pastors, plant new missions that become megachurches within a decade or less after that first public worship service, design a strategy that will attract younger adults to flock to our churches, and also serve as a prophetic and popular voice on highly divisive social, political, and religious issues.

In simple terms our problems are the product of inadequate human resources. It is true that many free agents in professional sports accept a lower compensation package in order to play with a team that appears to be a winner. They prefer that over a larger salary with a probable loser. A lot of twenty-nine-year-olds looking for their second job also prefer to sign up with a winner rather than a perceived loser. Winners do attract winners, and losers do attract the less gifted. Accepting that as inevitable, however, is a way to perpetuate the status quo, not to produce radical change!

This traveler is convinced W. Edwards Deming produced a better diagnostic conclusion: Systems produce the outcomes they are designed to produce.[5] Therefore, instead of blaming individuals for the numerical decline in the mainline Protestant denominations in recent decades, a more productive approach is to focus on how the system can be redesigned to produce desired outcomes. One reason to do that is the gradual replacement of the old clientele of 1955 with a new clientele.

A second reason is why did those buildings described in the opening paragraphs fall down. They collapsed because they were designed to serve a foreseeable set of circumstances. They were designed to fail when the unanticipated became the new reality. The denominational systems that were designed to serve the clientele of 1955 and to work in the cultural, social, religious, economic, and demographic context of that era have failed when the unanticipated became the new reality.

A third reason to focus on systems rather than personnel is it is at least three times as difficult to be an effective pastor today as it was in 1955. The changes in the expectations people bring to church plus the change in the context for ministry account for much of that. The rarely mentioned variable, however, is in 1955 the denominational system usually was a reliable and helpful ally. Today, by contrast, the larger the size of the congregation, the more likely the denominational system will be viewed as an adversary or as a competitor for resources, rather than as an ally.

This book has been written on the assumption that skyscrapers can and will be designed to survive the impact of a large commercial aircraft carrying a full load of passengers as well as a full load of fuel. This book has been written on the assumption that every one of those American Protestant denominations that has been experiencing numerical decline can reverse that trend. This is *not* whistling in the dark. This is not simply wishful thinking that the pendulum will begin to swing in the opposite direction. This is not based on a cyclical view of history. This optimistic assumption is based on four convictions. First, this pilgrim is *not* convinced that God has written off the mainline Protestant denominations as obsolete or irrelevant or redundant. Second, I am convinced we do know what must be done in order to produce a turnaround.

Third, I am convinced that for denominational systems to produce the desired outcomes in the twenty-first century, and to be able to do what we know must be done, will require radical changes in denominational systems including moving evangelism and missions to the top of the agenda.

Fourth, I am convinced we know how to do what must be done. This does not require learning from what worked back in the early 1950s. The focus must be on reaching adults born after 1960, not on those born before 1920! This means learning from what has worked for others in the late years of the twentieth century and early years of the twenty-first century. This distinction must drive the formulation of a larger strategy as well as in designing the various components of a turnaround strategy and in agreeing on the priorities in the allocation of scarce resources. The most highly visible example of this is in the launching of new missions. This distinction explains why new church development deserves a separate chapter.

Before exploring these consequences, it may be helpful to identify sixteen of the changes in the context for ministry in America that have made much of what worked in 1955 obsolete in 2005. This requires condensing what could be a book-length discussion into several pages. [6]

What Changed?

1. A New Religious Revival. While some will argue over whether it began in 1960 or 1965, few will dispute the impact of what has been described by Nobel Prize winner Robert William Fogel as "The Fourth Great Awakening."[7] When this latest religious revival is combined with a change in immigration patterns and an increase in the American population from 181 million in 1960 to a projected 300 million in 2011, one consequence is that every decade since 1960 has seen a new record established for worship attendance among white Protestant congregations, black Protestant churches, Asian-American congregations, and Latino churches. This has created a favorable context for any denomination seeking to expand its constituency. As Fogel points out, this fourth great religious revival also has fed the demand for a greater degree of egalitarianism in the American culture.

2. The Liberal-Evangelical Divide. Back in 1900 nearly all the Protestant denominations in America identified themselves as both evangelical and evangelistic. The *big* line of demarcation was between Roman Catholics and Protestants. The growth of the ecumenical movement in the second half of the twentieth century lowered that wall. The new influential line of demarcation finds evangelical Protestants on one side and liberal Protestants on the other side.[8] As recently as the 1950s, liberal and conservative Protestants often were united in opposition to a common enemy—Roman Catholicism.[9]

One consequence that goes back to 1965 is the Roman Catholic Church no longer is perceived as the common enemy, thus eliminating a rallying point for reinforcing cohesion. What is the replacement as a rallying point in your denomination?

During the past half century it is the evangelical wing of American Protestantism that has turned out to be the most effective in reaching adults born after 1950. That statement oversimplifies a more complex subject. An equally valid diagnostic statement is much of the recent numerical growth in the predominantly Anglo denominations in American Protestantism has occurred in congregations organized since 1960. The vast majority of these have been planted by evangelicals. Another equally valid diagnostic statement is a disproportionately large number of white Protestant churchgoers can be found in congregations that (a) were organized after 1960 and (b) now average more than 800 at worship. Again, most of these can be classified as "evangelical," including hundreds affiliated with a mainline Protestant denomination. Another valid diagnostic statement is a disproportionately large number of white Protestant churchgoers in America who were born after 1960 can be found in (a) nondenominational megachurches or (b) very large congregations affiliated with a denomination organized after 1906 such as the Assemblies of God.[10]

Finally, another relevant line of demarcation emerged in the late winter of 2003–2004 when Mel Gibson's film *The Passion of the Christ* received a variety of reviews. One group of Christians lamented the extensive violence and the absence of a greater emphasis on the love of God. A different perspective was articulated by those who focused on the suffering of Jesus. They pointed out that critical distinction between violence and suffering. Suffering is not a synonym for violence. They argued against what they perceived to be a "cross-less" version of Christianity.

The first group represented a theology focused on the first person of the Holy Trinity. The second group represented a focus on the second person of the Trinity.[11] That distinction is a crucial one in designing a turnaround strategy for your denomination. One example is if the predominantly Anglo denomination is seeking to become a multicultural religious body, most of the new missions may be organized to exalt either the second or third person of the Trinity. [12] Many of those Protestant congregations that include a disproportionately

21

large number of adults of Western European ancestry born after 1960 also usually focus on the second person of the Trinity.

At least a few of the old-timers who were reared in a denomination in the 1950s or 1960s that still retained a Western European heritage had been taught that the most meaningful lines of demarcation divided American Christianity into five categories: Anglican, Lutheran, Reformed, Roman Catholic, and "others." Decades later the Episcopal Church USA, the Evangelical Lutheran Church in America, the Presbyterian Church (USA), and the Reformed Church in America decided to come together in a new coalition. No one questioned the relevance of the first three sections of the Chicago Lambeth Quadrilateral of 1886 that was refined and endorsed by the Lambeth Conference of Anglican bishops two years later. At least a few Lutherans and Presbyterians, however, expressed reservations about the fourth section, which affirmed "The Historic Episcopate."

One consequence is that American churchgoers born after 1950 often place a much higher value on the theological stance of a prospective new church home than on the denominational affiliation of that congregation.

Another consequence is that the ecumenical movement not only has made it easier to switch allegiance across denominational lines, but also across that ancient Roman Catholic-Protestant line of demarcation. One result today is thousands of Protestant congregations organized around either the second or the third person of the Holy Trinity report substantial percentages of their new constituents were reared in the Roman Catholic Church. That pattern is even more pronounced in South America than in North America.

3. **Institutions Are Larger.** Whether the focus of the discussion is on medical clinics, universities, financial institutions, farms, grocery stores, major league professional sports, public high schools, what once were called variety stores and now are described as discount stores, municipal park sys-

tems, hospitals, or motion picture theaters, institutions in America are much larger today than they were in 1900 or 1950. That generalization also applies to Protestant congregations. The average (mean) size of a Protestant congregation in America today has more than doubled since 1900.

One consequence of the increase in the size of institutions has been an increased demand for specialists and fewer jobs for generalists. That trend can be seen in elementary schools, health care services, financial institutions, retail trade, military service, universities, journalism, agriculture, professional football, Protestant churches, as well as in denominational mergers that produced larger institutions. Specialties in the parish ministry include minister of missions, parish nurse, executive pastor, youth director, worship leader, media specialist, director of learning communities, church planter, and spiritual mentor. One consequence is a national marketplace is gradually replacing the regional marketplace in the search for staff. The national market increases the chances of finding a good match between the need and the candidate.

Another consequence is this has placed an impossible burden on theological schools. In 1920 medical school graduates left to practice their profession. Today most spend several more years as interns and residents before beginning private practice. Nearly all choose a specialty. Few are generalists.

In 1950 graduates of law schools left to practice law. Today a growing proportion of graduates devote several years to mastering a specialty, often on the staff of a large law firm or in the legal department of a large corporation.

In 1960 seminary graduates left school to become full-time parish pastors. That seminary degree was perceived to be adequate preparation for that assignment. Today a small but growing number of very large congregations that also serve as self-identified "teaching churches" are equipping adults for full-time positions as staff specialists in the parish ministry.

Perhaps the most significant consequence is only the very large congregations are able to mobilize the resources required to provide both the choices and the quality demanded by younger generations of churchgoers.

The attractiveness of economy of scale plus Biblical arguments made the twentieth century stand out as an era of denominational mergers. When that brought together two or more different polities or religious cultures or traditions, that encouraged compromises. One product of these compromises was a blurring of the denominational identity. A second was a major diversion of resources from ministry to institutional housekeeping.[13] A third is discussed in the next chapter.

Overlapping that is another unforeseen consequence. In choosing a pastor to lead in the creation of that growing number of very large American Protestant congregations, academic credentials often are viewed as less significant than was the pattern of the 1950s. Today that list of desirable qualities begins with passion, followed by high energy, skills as a visionary leader, a clearly and precisely defined Christian belief system, potential long tenure, an entrepreneurial personality, a healthy and happy marriage, skills in interpersonal relationships, experience on the staff of a megachurch, and academic credentials.

4. From Soloists to Quintets. For most of the history of American Protestantism, congregations had three choices. One was to share a minister with one or more other congregations. A second was to be served on a part-time basis by a bivocational minister or a student. The favorite, however, was to "have our own full-time resident pastor."

Theological schools usually focused on preparing students to serve as "the pastor" after graduation.

The demand today in the practice of medicine, of law, of education, and of ministry is for people who are both competent and comfortable serving as specialists and as members of a team.

One example of that change is that back in the 1950s and 1960s, a denominational board of missions sent a pastor out

24

to plant a new mission. A decade later most of those new missions either (a) had closed or (b) had plateaued with an average worship attendance of fewer than 150. One reason so many plateaued in size is they were designed to be served by a soloist, not by a team.

A common pattern today is to assemble a team of three to seven people, often including two or three part-time volunteers plus two or three full-time specialists. Their assignment is to plant a new mission that will be averaging at least 450 at worship twenty-four months after that first public worship service.

5. From Services to Experiences. In their book *The Experience Economy,* Pine and Gilmore point out that for most of human history the economy was organized around the gathering of commodities such as metals, wood, eggs, vegetables, hides, fruits, and petroleum. Gradually a growing proportion of the labor force focused on transforming commodities into goods: wheat into flour, cotton into clothing, hides into leather, and wood into furniture. The third stage in this evolving economy brought the rise of services. An increasing proportion of the labor force devoted their time and energy to providing other people with services such as transportation, communication, education, health care, legal and financial services, the distribution of goods (retail trade), and religious services. By the 1950s the service economy accounted for more than one-half of the jobs in the American economy. The most recent stage saw a rapidly growing number of Americans employed in producing meaningful and memorable experiences.[14] Amusement parks, rock climbing, entertainment, ocean cruises, enlisting volunteers as short-term missionaries to work in ministry with fellow Christians in a sister church on another continent, experiential learning, I-MAX® movies, and rock concerts are among the components of the contemporary American experience economy.

One consequence is to replace, or to supplement, that traditional worship service with interactive worship experiences. A second is to replace the old focus on Christian education and teaching with a new emphasis on learning. A third is the use of learning machines for customized individual experiences in working with children. A fourth is to replace that brief visit by a missionary on furlough who showed projected color slides to explain the work of missionaries with ten days as a volunteer short-term missionary working with fellow Christians in a sister church on another continent. A fifth is to volunteer to help launch a new worshiping community at that multisite church's fifth location rather than to send money to help finance a new denominationally sponsored mission.

Another obvious consequence is the change in expectations projected of midlevel and national denominational agencies.

6. **More Channels of Communication.** One of the two or three changes that have had the most profound impact on American Protestantism in recent years has been the expansion in the number and variety of channels of communication. As recently as 1950 the most widely used and influential channels of communication in the American culture were touch, the spoken word, facial expressions, eye contact, laughter, applause, physical gestures, music, the printed word, and photographs, including color slides and filmstrips.

Today the most powerful channels of communication may be touch, projected visual images, laughter, eye contact, facial expressions, applause, drawings, paintings, drama, video games, photographs, body language, the spoken word delivered in person, music, meaningful and memorable shared experiences, the spoken word delivered by projected visual images or telephone or e-mail, and the printed word.

One consequence is a change in the resources congregations seek from outside vendors, including denominational agencies.

7. **From Neighborhood to Regional.** Thanks to the combination of affluence, widespread private ownership of motor vehicles, cheap gasoline, and better roads, the journey from

home to work, to retail shopping, to recreation, to entertainment, to health care services, to visit close friends, to school, and to church has been getting longer. The 1950s were still organized around neighborhood institutions. School consolidation and that yellow bus have reduced the number of children who walk to school. The regional shopping center has replaced the retail stores on Main Street.

One consequence is the large regional church has been replacing the small-to-midsized neighborhood congregation that owned a one- or two-acre parcel of land. By contrast, that regional church allocates three to ten or more acres of land to interior streets and parking.

A related question arises when a congregation decides to relocate its meeting place or when a denomination decides to plant a new mission; *how much land should be purchased?* In 1955 the generous decision was three acres—one acre for parking, one acre for the building, and one acre for setbacks and landscaping.[15] By 1975 the prudent standard was ten acres. Today the answer is somewhere between twenty and three hundred acres, depending on whether the design is for a single site or a multisite congregation or to serve as a destination church.

One consequence is denominational leaders often are needed to encourage and advise vital congregations meeting in inadequate facilities on a small parcel of land to relocate their meeting place.

8. The Rising Costs of Pastors. In 1955 most American Protestant congregations could find a minister with a seminary degree who would serve as their full-time resident pastor at a cost of $3,000 to $4,000 annually, plus a church-owned house. In many parts of rural America that range was between $2,000 and $3,000, plus a house. That cost usually included the congregation's payment toward that minister's pension account and insurance on that church-owned house. The minister paid the utility bills as well as those for use of an automobile and medical, vision, and dental care, and subscriptions for periodicals and book purchases.

The costs to the congregation are higher today. That church-owned house usually is newer, larger, and more up-to-date. The monthly rental value may be fifteen to twenty times what it was in 1955. More and more congregations have decided to pay a housing allowance rather than to own and maintain a house. While exceptions exist, in addition to a cash salary, the congregation in 2005 typically will pay an additional $15,000 to $20,000 or more for their minister's health insurance, pension, car allowance, utilities, continuing education, and book allowance.

If an adjustment is made for inflation, the Consumer Price Index for 2005 will be approximately 7.2 times the index for 1955. That means $21,600 in 2005 will have the same buying power in the marketplace as $3,000 had in 1955—but that does not take into account the improvements in quality since 1955. Likewise $28,800 will have the equivalent purchasing power in 2005 as $4,000 had in 1955. The cost to a congregation of a church-owned house in 1955 plus $3,000 cash salary is equivalent in 2005 to $21,600 plus perhaps $18,000 for fringe benefits. That is close to double the increase in the Consumer Price Index.

In addition, back in 1955 the pastor's wife may have served as the unpaid "volunteer" church secretary. Today that congregation may pay $10,000 more or less for a part-time church secretary, plus that volunteer janitor has been replaced by a part-time paid custodian.

One consequence is a growing proportion of the congregations in American Protestantism have been priced out of the ministerial marketplace for a full-time and fully credentialed resident pastor. A second consequence is a shortage of seminary graduates with payments now due on the loans required for that seminary education who are willing to accept a call to a church paying a cash salary of $12,000 to $22,000 plus housing and other fringe benefits.

A third consequence is the combination of the need for specialized staff members and the rising costs of clergy have motivated the very large Protestant congregations to replace ordained generalists with lay specialists.

A fourth consequence is a growing number of small-to-midsized congregations have decided to affiliate with a large multisite congregation. This enables them to continue to enjoy the intimacy, the absence of complexity, and the spontaneity of the small church as well as continuing to worship in that place filled with sacred memories while also enjoying access to a variety of specialized ministries.[16]

9. The Drive for an Egalitarian Society. One of the most far-reaching changes of the past half century that has transformed American Protestantism has been the drive to create a more egalitarian society.[17] The highly visible components of this trend include the Civil Rights Movement, the move toward greater equality for women, the radical transformation of the culture of American military institutions, a greatly expanded role for the laity in the churches, the emergence of hundreds of nondenominational megachurches, an unprecedented emphasis in the profit-driven sectors of the American economy on customer service, a transformation of the relationships between physicians and patients, a sharp increase in the demand among homosexuals for equal rights, an increase in litigation, the replacement of the old vertical structures by horizontal partnerships (see chapter 2), changes in state laws on marriage, divorce, and parent-teenager disputes.

Among the consequences are several that will influence the design and implementation of a denominational turnaround strategy. One is the demand for the racial integration of the predominantly Anglo Protestant churches has been sidetracked by a demand for ethnic separation. This cry for ethnic separation is a response to maintaining complete local control.

A second consequence is the 1950s designs for new church development called for greater control by those providing the financial subsidies than is acceptable today.

A third consequence has been identified earlier—the gradual replacement of traditional vertical structures by horizontal partnerships. This can be seen in the growth of franchised retail establishments, the use of state-by-state party caucuses and primary elections in choosing a political party's nominee for the office of President of the United States, in the free-agency clause in player contracts in major league professional sports, in ad hoc coalitions of congregations of similar types, size, and/or priorities affiliated with various denominations, in the rapid increase in the number and variety of caucuses and organized interest groups in several Protestant denominations, in agricultural cooperatives, and in that new era of affinity partnerships in American Protestantism.

For those who believe Christian congregations should focus on the transformation of people's lives, an important consequence of egalitarianism has been an amendment to the 1950s plan for congregations to send money to hire people to do ministry on their behalf on other continents. The egalitarian model calls for American congregations to build direct church-to-church relationships with sister congregations in other parts of the world. In addition to sending money, the American congregations send short-term volunteer missionaries to work in ministry with fellow Christians in those sister churches.

One bonus is the American churches sent volunteers who often return as transformed believers. A second bonus comes when that American congregation welcomes volunteers in ministry from their sister church who come to America to partner in doing ministry here.

A fourth consequence often is described as "disengagement."[18] An increasing proportion of the laity is becoming disengaged from the denominational system with which their congregation is affiliated. One expression of that disengagement is the relative ease with which many churchgoers born after 1960 switch their religious affiliation from one Protestant tradition to another or from Catholic to Protestant. Another expression of disengagement is the increased difficulty in persuading members to rally together in support of a denominational goal.

A fifth consequence emerges when disengagement is transformed into alienation. The nineteenth century in American Protestantism was marked by scores of schisms that created new denominations. The twentieth century was marked by reunions and mergers. Will the twenty-first bring a new wave of schisms? That growing demand for self-rule has sparked what may turn out to be a wave of schisms among the mainline Protestant denominations.[19] The Presbyterians, who often lead the way with other denominations two or three decades behind, experienced two schisms that produced new denominations in 1973 and 1981. Will others follow?

During the middle third of the nineteenth century the Methodists, Baptists, and Presbyterians experienced a high level of intradenominational quarreling that led to schisms.[20] While no one can prove cause and effect, once the schisms had become history, most of the resulting denominations were free to rally support for that huge wave of new church development that followed the Civil War. Could schism pave the road to replace intradenominational quarreling in your denomination with a new unifying focus on evangelism? Would that eliminate the internal quarreling in your denomination and free the leaders to concentrate on designing and implementing a turnaround strategy? For five or six of the ten largest Protestant denominations in America the right answer probably is no! For four or five, however, the time may have arrived to give division serious consideration by weighing the trade-offs. Or should the first priority be to recreate a sense of unity that will nurture denominational loyalty? What could be the cause, or the common enemy, that would serve as a rallying point to create a new sense of unity? (See the last few pages of chapter 7.)

10. The Change in Immigration Patterns. The steamships that brought venturesome immigrants to the United States from Europe have been replaced by commercial aircraft that bring venturesome immigrants from the Pacific Rim and the predators who guide the poor but ambitious from Latin America to the promised land.

One consequence is a new wave of immigrant congregations. The Norwegian Lutherans, the Italian Methodists, the German Reformed, the Swedish Baptists, and the Dutch Reformed congregations of the 1920s have become Americanized. The Hispanic Baptists, the Korean Presbyterians, the Japanese Methodists, and the Chinese Lutherans symbolize a new wave of immigrant churches.

This raises a crucial question in designing a turnaround strategy for your denomination. Do you want to transform what has been a denomination consisting largely of people with a Western European ancestry into a multicultural religious body? If yes, how do you respond to the pressures for ethnic separation and self-rule? One alternative is to adopt a goal of becoming a multicultural denomination consisting of a collection of monocultural affinity midlevel judicatories.[21]

A second alternative is to create a collection of nongeographical multicultural midlevel judicatories. Each judicatory would be designed to include largely or completely monocultural congregations with perhaps a score or more consisting of Asian-American churches, another dozen or more of African-American congregations, perhaps two dozen Latino churches, two or three dozen predominantly Anglo churches, plus a score or more representing other ethnic minorities. A reasonable goal would be that each midlevel judicatory would include approximately one hundred churches. The long-term goal would be Anglo congregations would be a minority in at least one-half of these midlevel judicatories by 2025.

A third alternative could be to create a multicultural denomination consisting of geographically defined regional judicatories consisting largely of multicultural congregations.[22] The long-term goal could be for each congregation to include a significant number of members from each of three or more ethnic groups in order to minimize the possibilities that any one ethnic group would constitute a majority of the members of that congregation. This can be accomplished in communities with a diverse multicultural population, but it usually requires a very long pastorate by an exceptionally gifted senior minister.

11. The Demand for Accountability. One product of the combination of egalitarianism, the shift from vertical hierarchies to horizontal partnerships, and the feeding of the fires of adversarial relationships has been a greater demand for accountability. This can be seen in the profit-driven sectors of the American economy, in the delivery of health care services, in the criticisms of the public schools, in the practices of tax-exempt foundations, in the manufacture and sale of tobacco products, in journalism, in denominational systems organized on a hierarchical model, in the conduct of American foreign policy, and in the expenditure of charitable contributions.

The expressions of this demand for greater accountability have substantially undermined the assumptions on which many denominational systems of 1955 were based. One, as explained earlier in this chapter, was an affirmation of unified budgets and recipient-driven contributions. That began to be challenged after World War II as denominations launched special appeals for "second mile" contributions for relief of the victims of the war, for new church development, and for other causes. As the decades rolled past and new egalitarianism blossomed, contributors began to conclude, "I believe I know better than anyone else what would be the best final destination for my charitable contributions." That old recipient-driven system continued to work in those religious bodies that perceived themselves to be high commitment covenant communities based on legal principles as described in chapter 2. The combination of the calendar, affluence, and millions of funerals, however, increased the number committed to donor-designated contributions.

A second expression was the purchase of goods and services by congregations. In the 1950s most congregations expressed their loyalty by turning to their denomination for many goods and services. During the past forty years, however, the growing demand for relevance, quality, customized services and products, creativity, new approaches, and economy has led many congregations to purchase these goods and services from parachurch organizations, theological schools, state universities, profit-driven corporations, megachurches, retreat centers, and independent entrepreneurs.

One obvious consequence of that trend has been an erosion of denominational loyalty. Today institutional loyalty is rarely inherited. It must be earned and earned again via excellence in customer service.

Reinforcing this erosion of denominational loyalty and supporting the demand for greater accountability have been the shift from vertical hierarchies to horizontal partnerships and the growth of egalitarianism.

One consequence is the design of a denominational turnaround strategy should include criteria, benchmarks, and mileposts that can be used to measure progress when demands for accountability are addressed to those responsible for the implementation of that strategy. That will require devoting as much attention to defining the desired outcomes as is given to describing and mobilizing the necessary inputs into that process.

A related consequence is the need to include the creation of partnerships for the implementation of that turnaround strategy.

One motivation for a positive response to this demand for accountability is to quiet internal discontent and to thwart the drift toward disengagement. A better motivation, however, is to recognize and affirm that accountability is an essential component of any effort to raise the level of performance. That generalization applies to any organization created to produce desirable outcomes. That includes profit-driven corporations, charitable foundations, public schools, congregations, professional sports teams, prisons, political parties, and denominational systems.

12. The Decline of Civility. Every major change carries a price tag. The combination of egalitarianism, the increase in civil litigation, the proliferation of adversarial relationships, and the demand for accountability plus an affirmation of investigative reporting by journalists and the decrease in respect for persons in positions of authority by virtue of their office (police officers, presidents, governors, mayors, bishops, physicians, clergypersons, university professors, department heads, bankers, classroom teachers, et al.) have produced a decline in civility. [23] This has had many consequences. One is attack ads on rival candidates in political campaigns. Another has been an erosion of one source of internal denominational cohesion that was still powerful in the 1950s.

13. The Arrival of the Internet. A persuasive argument could be made that the Internet should be placed first on this list of influential recent changes that have altered the context for ministers. What did denominations do in the 1950s? They provided resources for congregations and pastors, assisted in the placement of ministers, helped people about to change their address search for a new church home, encouraged Christians to participate in prayer groups, and enabled church members to stay in communication with missionaries on other continents. These and dozens of other services are now available on the Web—and that is only the beginning of that story.

14. From Sending to Receiving Missionaries. Perhaps the least widely discussed of any of these sixteen changes is the presence of an estimated thirty thousand missionaries in the United States sent here by religious bodies on other continents. Most, but not all, are Christians. Many came to organize and lead new worshiping communities consisting of immigrants to the United States from Ghana or Korea or Nigeria or India or Mexico or Taiwan or some other country.

This raises a question on staffing new missions designed to reach recent immigrants. How large is the pool from which you select your mission developers?

15. How Do Americans Identify Themselves? For those American Protestant denominations that represent a Western European religious heritage, one of the most influential books of the post–World War II era was *Protestant, Catholic, Jew* by Will Herberg.[24] Herberg's basic thesis was that for more than half a century residents of the United States had classified themselves by their nationality: German, Swedish, Italian, and so on. He argued in this book that Americans in the 1950s were using a new system of self-identification. This was religion. The political campaigns for the office of President of the United States in 1928 and 1960 supported Herberg's thesis.

Five of the most significant changes since Herberg wrote are (1) the internal harmony and sense of unity within both the Roman Catholic Church in America and most of the larger Protestant denominations has been replaced by quarreling, litigation, and adversarial relationships, (2) the primary allegiance of millions of younger American Christians is to their congregation and/or their pastor, not to their denomination, (3) interfaith and interdenominational marriages are far more common today then Herberg anticipated, (4) in many communities a large proportion of the Protestant megachurches are not affiliated with any of the mainline Protestant denominations, and (5) Herberg did not anticipate the arrival of tens of millions of immigrants who have come to America since 1955.

16. Does Entertainment Drive the American Culture? This is placed last because it may be the most divisive. One perspective is based on the dictionary definition of the word "entertain." As Pastor Walt Kallestad pointed out several years ago, one of the first definitions is "to show hospitality to." That led Pastor Kallestad to design a ministry called "Entertainment Evangelism." The central theme called for congregations to greet, welcome, and show hospitality to strangers and first-time visitors. When a brief description of this plan was published in *The Lutheran*, it evoked a flood of negative responses. Christian churches are called to proclaim the Gospel of Jesus Christ, not to be entertainment centers!

Many years later similar criticisms are directed at congregations that use projected visual imagery or praise music or liturgical dance in worship. In the secular world similar criticisms are directed at university professors who give entertaining lectures or television anchor teams who have fun while delivering the evening news or candidates for elective political office who are entertaining personalities or restaurants that provide entertainment with their meals or television commercials designed to entertain the viewers or the entertainment that interrupts the university football game at half time or fundraisers who entertain prospective donors or field trips for seventh graders that are described as "a waste of a school day to entertain bored kids" or colleges that entertain high school seniors who are potential future students or the football player who seeks to entertain the crowd after scoring a touchdown.[25]

One consequence of an entertainment-driven culture has been the creation of a new definition of acceptable Christian music. Another is an increasing acceptance of the definition of meaningful, relevant, and memorable worship as "good theater." A third is the use of drama in proclaiming the Gospel.

What will be the role of entertainment in your turnaround strategy? More specifically, if your strategy includes an emphasis on creating congregations that either (a) display the characteristics of a closely knit community or (b) consist of a collection of closely knit small communities, what will be the central organizing principles that provide the cohesion to glue those communities together? What is the glue that holds the members of that weekly quilting circle together? What are the cohesive forces that glue that adult vocal choir together? Does entertainment represent "pandering to the popular culture"? Or is it an acceptable part of a larger strategy to proclaim the Gospel to younger generations?

What's the Point?

This is far from an exhaustive review of the changes in the context for "doing church in twenty-first-century America."

These are, however, among the most influential. If the focus were solely on preaching, for example, we would have added the emergence of the therapeutic culture. One consequence has been the creation of lay-staffed "hot lines" and lay-led mutual support groups to challenge the old expert-dominated systems in providing aid to troubled individuals.[26] Another consequence that became popular after World War II were sermons that resembled the central theme of a group counseling session. Another was preaching that focused on God's love, but rarely referred to God.[27] One result was the messenger became the message. That helped erode the traditional loyalties that were so influential in the 1950s, but were not inherited by many of the churchgoers born after 1950.

The combined impact of these and other changes can be summarized in two words: *increased competition*. The past four decades have brought a dramatic increase in the level of competition all across the American economy. Examples include commercial air travel, the sale of groceries, the pursuit of the charitable dollar, and the discretionary time of individuals. One consequence has been the erosion of community as Americans focused on individual goals.[28]

A long-term perspective does reveal that the competition among the churches in the United States goes back nearly two hundred years, but the mainline Protestant denominations dominated the center of the stage through the 1950s.[29]

How can we explain the decline of the mainline denominations that dominated American Protestantism in the 1950s? One explanation is the change in the context and the arrival of younger generations have made those old systems obsolete. The winners of the 1800–1950 era have become the losers of the post-1950 competition.[30] A disproportionately large number of the winners since 1950 have come from among the newer denominations and movements and the nondenominational independent churches. A more useful diagnosis suggests the mainline Protestant denominations are no longer competitive.

What Have Been the Recent Outcomes?

The population of the United States increased by more than 100 million between 1960 and 2000. That rising tide saw several denominations enjoy a huge increase in membership while others experienced net losses. One way to describe that is to look at the ratio of members to population.

The most comprehensive census of religious bodies ever completed in the United States was taken in 1906 by the United States Bureau of the Census. [31] It revealed that one out of 40 residents of the United States was a member of one of the two dozen Lutheran denominations in America. One in 16 was a member of one of the six predecessor denominations that have constituted The United Methodist Church since 1968. One in 98 was a member of one of the three big Negro Methodist denominations. One in 96 was a member of the Protestant Episcopal Church. One in 65 was a member of one of the four predecessor bodies of what in 1957 became the United Church of Christ. One in 46 was a member of one of the twelve Presbyterian denominations. One in 86 was a member of the Christian Church (Disciples of Christ). One in seven was a baptized Roman Catholic. One in 81 was a member of the Northern Baptist congregation. One in 36 was a member of the National Baptist Convention. One in 44 was a Southern Baptist. One in 680 was a member of the Reformed Church in America while one in 3,400 was a member of the Christian Reformed Church. One in 630 was a member of the predecessor bodies of what today is the Unitarian Universalist Association. One in 325 was a Mormon. One in 1,350 was a Seventh-day Adventist. One in 750 was a Quaker and one in 115 was a member of an independent or nondenominational congregation. (The methodology suggests an undercount of independent churches.)

The following table summarizes the changes in several religious traditions during the twentieth century. Several religious traditions experienced a decrease in their "market share" of the American population that increased by nearly 200 million during those 94 years. That list includes the American Baptists, the Disciples of Christ, the Episcopal Church, Lutherans, Presbyterians, Quakers (Friends), the Unitarian Universalist Association, The United Methodist Church, and the United Church of Christ.

The big omission from this table is the product of an absence of historical data. A reasonable guess, however, is the combined "market share" of all of the independent or nondenominational Protestant congregations in America has increased from perhaps one constituent for every 300 residents in 1953 to one in ten today.

Table 1

Ratios of Baptized Membership to U.S. Population

DENOMINATION	1906 RATIO	1953 RATIO[32]	2000 RATIO
American Baptist Churches	1 in 81	1 in 103	1 in 160
Assemblies of God	N.A.	1 in 430	1 in 110
Baptist General Conference	N.A.	1 in 3,200	1 in 2,000
Christian and Missionary Alliance	N.A.	1 in 2,860	1 in 770
Christian Reformed Church	1 in 3,400	1 in 820	1 in 1,130
Church of the Nazarene	N.A.	1 in 640	1 in 445
Disciples of Christ	1 in 86	1 in 86	1 in 345
Episcopal Church USA	1 in 96	1 in 63	1 in 125
Evangelical Covenant Church	N.A.	1 in 3,077	1 in 1,840
Evangelical Free Church	N.A.	1 in 5,715	1 in 1,160
Three Black Methodist Denominations	1 in 98	N.A.	1 in 61
Latter-day Saints (Mormons)	1 in 395	1 in 148	1 in 68
Lutherans (all)	1 in 40	1 in 22	1 in 33

National Baptist Convention, Inc.	1 in 36	N.A.	1 in 80
Presbyterians (all)	1 in 46	1 in 44	1 in 75
Quaker (Friends)	1 in 750	1 in 1,400	1 in 1,600
Reformed Church in America	1 in 680	1 in 810	1 in 970
Roman Catholic Church	1 in 7	1 in 5	1 in 4.5
Seventh-day Adventist Church	1 in 1,350	1 in 610	1 in 303
Southern Baptist Convention	1 in 44	1 in 20	1 in 15
Unitarian-Universalist Association	1 in 630	1 in 1,000	1 in 1,540
United Methodist Church	1 in 16	1 in 16	1 in 27
United Church of Christ	1 in 65	1 in 75	1 in 165
Wisconsin Evangelical Lutheran Synod	N.A.	1 in 505	1 in 390

On the other side of the ledger, several denominations increased their share of the churchgoing population. That list includes the Christian Reformed Church, the Evangelical Covenant Church, the Evangelical Free Church, the Church of Jesus Christ of Latter-day Saints (Mormons), the Seventh-day Adventists, the Southern Baptists, and, of course, the Assemblies of God who were organized in 1914.

CAUTION: These numbers are not as precise as they first appear. The definition of "member" not only varies from one religious tradition to another, but also may not be consistent over a long period of time. The definition used here is "inclusive," which usually includes baptized as well as confirmed members. One limitation arises when a member drops out but no letter of transfer is issued. In 2002, for example, the Roman Catholic Church in America reported a total of approximately 65 million baptized members. Membership audits conducted in several dioceses suggested at least 15 million of those 65 million had either (a) dropped out of church completely or (b) joined a Protestant congregation. Those audits suggest one out of six Americans is a baptized member of a Roman Catholic parish rather than one out of four or five.

The First Step

If your denomination is seriously interested in reaching, attracting, serving, nurturing, assimilating, and challenging the generations of Americans born after 1960, what do you do? A productive first step could be to identify and examine the outcomes your denominational system produced during the twentieth century. Do the congregations affiliated with your denomination include a larger or a smaller proportion of the population than was the pattern in earlier periods of the twentieth century?

If you are satisfied with that relatively simple definition of the outcomes, you may decide to focus on continuing to do what you have been doing. If you are dissatisfied, you may decide to undertake a more extensive audit of past performance.

A Possible Second Step

Long-term trends often reveal more than does a one-time spot check; therefore, if the data can be gathered, a useful performance audit could consist of three parts. One would cover the most recent reporting year. A second part could summarize performance over the past ten years. The third part could summarize these data over either the past three or four decades or for the period beginning with the first year following the most recent denominational merger through the last full reporting year. For the Evangelical Lutheran Church in America, for example, that audit could compare last year with 1988, 1993, 1998, and 2003.

Among the questions asked in that annual performance audit, these three dozen could be among the most revealing:

1. Combined total average worship attendance of all congregations.
2. Number of confirmed members.
3. Number of baptized members.
4. Annual death rate among confirmed members.
5. New members received.
6. New members received by intradenominational transfers.
7. Baptisms (all ages).
8. Number of congregations.
9. Number of new missions holding first public worship service.
10. Number of congregations dissolved or closed.
11. Number of congregations merged with another congregation.
12. Number of congregations that relocated their meeting place.
13. Number of congregations scheduling two or more worship services every weekend.
14. Number of congregations scheduling weekend worship at two or more locations every weekend.
15. Average Sunday school attendance.
16. Number of congregations averaging 800 or more at worship.
17. Number of congregations averaging 500-799 at worship.
18. Number of congregations averaging 350-499 at worship.
19. Number of congregations averaging 150-349 at worship.
20. Number of congregations averaging 100-149 at worship.
21. Number of congregations averaging 75-99 at worship. (One-half of all congregations in American Protestantism report an average worship attendance of 80 or fewer.)

22. Number of congregations averaging 50-74 at worship.
23. Number of congregations averaging 1-49 at worship.
24. Proportion of congregations in each of those eight size categories that reported an increase of 5 percent or more over the previous year in average worship attendance.
25. Proportion of congregations in each of those eight categories that reported the number of new members received last year exceeded 8 percent of reported membership at close of previous reporting year.
26. Number of congregations served by one or more full-time and fully credentialed pastors.
27. Proportion of pastors or senior ministers who have completed at least twenty years with same congregation.
28. Proportion of pastors or senior ministers who have completed at least ten years with same congregation.
29. Proportion of full-time and fully credentialed parish pastors who have chosen to retire before age 65.
30. Number of senior ministers of congregations averaging 500 or more at worship who are not graduates of an accredited theological school.
31. Number of senior ministers of congregations averaging 500 or more at worship who are graduates of a seminary not related to your denomination.
32. Combined grand total of congregational receipts received from living donors in last reporting year.
33. Combined grand total of congregational receipts received from all sources last year.
34. Proportion of above that was sent to your regional judicatories and national treasuries.
35. Total expenditures by all congregations for all benevolences and denominational causes.

36. Total expenditures by congregations for capital improvements.

These should be seen only as suggestions, and the actual wording of many may have to be adapted to fit the polity and traditions of your denomination. In several denominations this will require a revision of the annual report form completed by each congregation. Several of these questions provide useful one-time information. Overall, however, the greatest value lies in being able to identify long-term trends.

The value of collecting these statistical reports can be greatly enhanced by an annual mailing to each congregation that includes the data for each question for the past several years for that congregation plus how that congregation ranks when compared with other churches on questions 1-7, 13-28, and 32-36.

After the computer software has been designed to collect, order, and store these data, it will be relatively easy to print out a customized statistical report for each congregation every year. The information specialist on the staff of the midlevel judicatory or appropriate national agency may want to add a couple of hundred words to each congregational report identifying the most significant trends for that congregation and concluding with a couple of "How do you interpret that?" type of questions.

After five or six years of collecting, reporting, and interpreting these data, one result probably will be 20 percent of the value of the effort will be in resourcing denominational planning and policy-making while 80 percent of the value will be in resourcing the planning and decision-making processes in congregations.

That *Big* Step

The most significant step in the early stages of designing a customized turnaround strategy for your denomination that is compatible with the American religious, social, and economic realities of the twenty-first century is the theme of this chapter. That begins with reaching agreement on the top priorities among the desired outcomes your denominational system is expected to produce during the next several years. That list of possibilities could include, based on the record of recent decades in several mainline Protestant denominations, (1) another denominational merger, (2) increasing the degree of polarization among the members, (3) increasing the number of very large congregations, (4) reducing the number of affiliated congregations, (5) increasing the number of very small churches, (6) raising more money for denominational budgets, (7) promoting ecumenism, (8) transforming an American religious body into a global church, (9) withdrawing from the large central cities and older suburbs in the North, (10) planting a larger number of new missions, (11) transferring financial resources from larger congregations to smaller churches, or (12) reaching, attracting, serving, nurturing, assimilating, and challenging the generations of American-born residents born after 1960 as well as recent immigrants from other parts of this planet. (We are leaving to God the responsibility to reach residents of other planets in other galaxies.)

If agreement is reached that number 12 tops the list of desired outcomes for your denominational system in the years ahead, that will require redesigning your denominational system if it has not been producing that outcome. That can be done! This will require building a denominational system that is compatible with the American context for doing ministry in the twenty-first century. What worked so well in the context of 1955 may have to be replaced. The first step, as emphasized earlier, is to gain widespread agreement on the number one desired outcome. Is reaching the generations born after 1960 the top priority? Or is taking better care of today's constituents the number one goal? Or are institutional maintenance goals at the top of that list? Or perpetuating a denominational system that worked so well in the 1950s?

If agreement is reached on the identity of that number one constituency, what will be the most effective way to reach them? To plant new missions that plateau in size with an average worship attendance of 150 or fewer? Or to increase the number of megachurches in your denomination? Or to increase the number of churches averaging fewer than fifty at worship? Or to increase the number of midsized churches? Or to encourage long pastorates? Or to encourage the emergence of more multisite churches?

The obvious temptation is to focus on those operational policies. A more productive approach will require backing off and focusing on five other questions. First, who will be the partners who will be enlisted to help design and implement a turnaround strategy? Will these partners be drawn largely from the staff and board members of the national denominational agencies? Or from the staff and board members of the midlevel judicatories? Or from the ministerial and lay leadership of large and numerically growing congregations that have been attracting large numbers of adults born after 1960? Or from leaders in affiliated congregations that have been most effective in reaching and serving ethnic minorities and recent immigrants? Or will you decide to outsource the design of a comprehensive strategy?

Second, if your denomination has been experiencing several years of numerical decline, is this due, at least in part, to the fact that the American religious scene has become a far more competitive ecclesiastical free market than it was back in the 1950s? If you agree that is part of the agenda, what changes will be required for your denomination to become more competitive?

Third, what diagnostic clues can be gleaned from an analysis of those audits of performance described earlier?

Fourth, what are the barriers that must be identified and removed before a constructive course of action can be initiated?

Among the most common barriers are denial; an overloaded denominational agenda; an obsolete or dysfunctional denominational system that makes it difficult to reach agreement on priorities; an increasingly polarized constituency on issues of control, doctrine, polity, social and political issues, and denominational priorities; the power of tradition; the temptation to assume that one size will fit all rather than affirming the value of customized plans in designing that turnaround strategy; the natural tendency of any large bureaucracy to defend itself and its past rather than to embrace reform; disagreement over what the future will bring; and the natural institutional tendency to fund entitlements created in the past rather than to evaluate actual performance.

Which Rule Book?

Finally, what will be the nature of the rule book that will be used to guide denominational policies and practices in the years ahead? Three popular sports today are soccer, basketball, and baseball. Each one is played by a different rule book. Nonprofit agencies play by a different rule book than is used by profit-driven corporations. The successful farmer of today uses a different rule book than the one granddad followed back in 1935.

For this discussion three different types of rule books are in use today in American Christianity. One is utilized by a growing number of Protestant congregations, both nondenominational and denominationally related, that have been remarkably effective in reaching, attracting, serving, nurturing, assimilating, and challenging the generations born after 1960. One section of their rule book, to quote from one of these congregations, reads, "Our ministry is driven by a passion to help people find hope, meaning, and new life through Jesus Christ." The rule books followed by these congregations focus on the transformation of people's lives. That is the name of their game.

Another section makes it clear that the policies and decisions that create that customized ministry are initiated and approved by local leadership. In some cases these may require denominational approval, but that approval usually is easy to secure since it travels across a bridge constructed out of mutual trust.

This rule book currently is being followed by a growing number of nondenominational megachurches founded since 1960. It also is being used in thousands of Presbyterian, Lutheran, United Methodist, Episcopal, Baptist, United Church of Christ, and other denominationally affiliated congregations.

A second, but somewhat similar rule book, is followed in those denominational systems that closely resemble a voluntary association. A third rule book is used in those American Christian bodies that were designed to be high expectation, high commitment covenant communities based on clearly defined and widely accepted legal principles.

The differences between those last two rule books are critically important in designing a relevant and productive denominational system for the institutional expression of the Christian faith in twenty-first-century America. That explains why that issue deserves a separate chapter.

CHAPTER TWO

WHICH RULE BOOK?

Several years ago the elders of a midsized nondenominational Protestant congregation publicly rebuked a member for sexual misconduct. Subsequently she sued the elders in civil court for defamation of character. The elders explained and defended their action. They had been elected to oversee both the belief system and the behavior of the members. If a member made public statements contrary to the teachings of that congregation, the elders were obligated to reprimand that member and to correct those heretical statements. Likewise, if a member engaged in unacceptable behavior, the elders were obligated to reprimand the offending member. They also stated that when she had been admitted into membership, this member publicly accepted the oversight of the elders over both doctrine and behavior.

This unhappy member replied that she had accepted the oversight of the elders when she was accepted into membership, but that relationship had been terminated when she submitted her letter of resignation. The public rebuke by the elders had been delivered long after that letter of resignation had been submitted.

The elders explained to the court their congregation was a high commitment covenant community organized on the basis of a shared commitment. Every candidate for membership had to be examined by the elders to be sure that person

51

understood, agreed with, and supported the contents of that shared commitment that covered both doctrine and behavior. Likewise, a request to terminate one's membership had to be approved by the elders. Since that approval of termination had not occurred when the public rebuke was issued, she was still a member and therefore still under the oversight of the elders.

That litigation illustrated two of the most significant lines of demarcation in designing and implementing a turnaround strategy for your denomination. That first line is the distinction between the religious body that is designed as a voluntary association of congregations, midlevel judicatories, the clergy, national agencies, and other institutions such as church-related colleges, theological schools, publishing houses, and denominationally owned camps and homes on the one hand, and on the other hand, those religious bodies that are high expectation, high commitment covenant communities united by clearly stated and widely affirmed legal principles. Those organizing principles call for two different rule books. The rule book governing the operation of a voluntary association differs greatly from the rule book followed in the high commitment covenant community.

The second big line of demarcation distinguishes between the current constituents who believe the denomination should function as a high expectation, high commitment covenant community based on clearly defined legal principles and those who believe it should operate as a voluntary association. A common source of divisive internal conflict and unfilled hopes in contemporary American Protestantism emerges when one group of today's leaders operates on the assumption this is a voluntary association while others are convinced it is a covenant community organized under legal principles.[1]

What's the Difference?

A simple but fallible indicator is to compare the combined average worship attendance of all congregations with the combined membership, age fourteen and over. If the combined average worship attendance exceeds the confirmed membership, this probably is a high expectation religious body. If that ratio is below 60 percent, it probably is a voluntary association of low to midlevel expectation congregations.

In congregational terms, the voluntary associations usually have a low threshold into full membership. In the high expectation covenant communities, that is a high threshold and presented as a two-way covenant. One common consequence of that high threshold is newcomers must be regular participants in the corporate worship of God in that congregation for at least a year before they are eligible to begin the process of preparing to become a member. Another is a majority of the worshipers are adults who are unwilling or unable to meet the high standards required for membership. They come to be spiritually fed, but they are not ready to cross that high threshold into membership.

Policy planning, which is the model usually followed in designing a turnaround strategy for a denomination, is especially difficult when the congregational perspective suggests this is a voluntary association organized around a shared commitment to evangelism and missions while the denominational leaders may act on the assumption it is a covenant community based on legal principles. One limited example of that is the United Church of Christ. With a few exceptions, the Constitution of the United Church of Christ (UCC) suggests this is a voluntary association of congregations, associations, conferences, national agencies, and other institutions. One point of confusion is the right of withdrawal. To become a member, a congregation has to submit a request. That request for membership has to be approved by the appropriate association. If a conference does not include associations, approval of that request for membership must be made by the conference. That is a two-party or bilateral process. Can a congregation unilaterally withdraw its membership? That right of unilateral withdrawal is a central characteristic of voluntary associations.

The big reservation about describing the United Church of Christ as a voluntary association, however, is that the UCC also is a religious organization. That introduces another factor. The UCC is a voluntary association in institutional terms, but as its constitution makes clear, it also is a Christian religious body with a covenantal theology and a shared commitment to evangelism and missions. This is a *crucial* distinction! Unlike such religious bodies in the Roman Catholic Church, The United Methodist Church, and the Episcopal Church USA, which are organized around an internally shared commitment to doctrine, polity, and governance as well as to evangelism and missions, the UCC resembles a voluntary association on Biblical interpretation and governance. Another modest exception is control over ministerial standing rests with the association, not with the congregation.

Those American religious bodies that are purely voluntary associations usually do not identify themselves as a "church"—that word is reserved for congregations. That emphasis on covenantal theology plus the shared focus on evangelism and missions, but not on control over local leadership, helps to explain why the UCC should identify itself as a church, rather than an association or convention or fellowship or movement or society. The Christian religious body that is truly a voluntary association does not use the word "church" in its name.

That introduces a second example of this definition of a voluntary association in general and that unilateral right of withdrawal in particular. Southern Baptists, who identify themselves as a convention, not as a church, have been spending hundreds of thousands of dollars in recent years on litigation in civil courts contesting the right of withdrawal. In that American religious tradition, which has been influenced by the individualism nurtured on the frontier, one school of thought contends that the polity, history, and traditions of the Southern Baptist Convention (SBC) are consistent with the contention it is a voluntary association of congregations, associations, regional conventions, and a variety of other institutions. Therefore each congregation is completely autonomous on matters of doctrine, polity, and practices (such as the ordination of women). That perspective also can be used to support the right of every association or regional convention to reject the application by congregations for membership or to terminate the membership of a congregation. That perspective also supports the argument that every SBC-related college, seminary, retreat center, home, publishing house, or other SBC-related institution has the right to be governed by its own self-perpetuating board of directors rather than by a board consisting of directors elected by the denomination.

On the other side are those who believe the SBC is a high commitment covenant community organized around a collection of legal principles. These legal principles grant considerable control and oversight to the duly elected officials of various national and regional agencies. That includes granting the state convention the authority to choose the members of the governing boards of affiliated organizations. That also may include the right to require paid staff persons to sign an affirmation of a specific theological or ideological statement. Agreement with that central doctrinal statement is a common characteristic of the covenant community. In fact, for many covenant communities a signed affirmation of that statement is a requirement for voting membership.

The most highly visible example of the importance assigned to that theological statement is every candidate for ordination must take a vow to uphold that doctrinal statement in order to be ordained. In The United Methodist Church (UMC), for example, that doctrinal statement, called "The Articles of Religion," is a part of the denomination's constitution. While that doctrinal statement can be amended, it is highly unlikely the supermajority required for amending it can be achieved. One consequence is a highly divisive internal quarrel within The United Methodist Church over whether an ordained minister is required to uphold and obey the law of that church—and it is a church not a convention or association—and to faithfully and accurately teach the doctrinal position articulated in the constitution of that church. If the UMC is a voluntary association, the clergy should be free to ignore both the law and the doctrinal position of that religious body. If it is high commitment religious body organized on the basis of church law, the clergy are bound by their vows to obey the law of that church in which they were ordained.

In many American religious bodies an affirmation of that central doctrinal statement not only is a requirement for ordination, it also is a requirement for any lay person seeking to become a full member of an affiliated congregation.

Thus the common characteristics of the covenant community organized around legal principles in American Christianity include (1) a precisely worded belief system, (2) a clearly stated reason for the existence of that institution, (3) a statement of the expectations projected of those who seek to become members or may be called to serve as official leaders, (4) a written constitution covering both doctrine and polity that is difficult to amend, (5) standards of behavior required of all members, (6) a system for disciplining members, and (7) a clearly defined point in the organizational structure to which appeals of decision can be directed.

As the decades roll by, normal, natural, and predictable institutional pressures tend to move these human associations organized around legal principles in the direction of affirming and strengthening a centralized command and control system of governance. A parallel pattern is the internal battle over control moves above fulfilling the original purpose in the allocation of time, energy, creativity, and money. Likewise the longer that original constitution has been in force and/or the larger the number of paid national and regional staff, the more likely conflict will surface over both the meaning and the application of "our rules." A second natural institutional tendency surfaces when a scarcity of resources requires rationing those scarce resources. As the decades roll by, the tendency is to make fulfilling that original purpose a secondary priority and moving care of the institution to the top of the list.

If we divide human associations into two categories, one organized as a high commitment covenant community governed by a set of legal principles and a second created as a voluntary association of people drawn together by a shared interest, the differences become clearer. The shared interest that motivates people to join what they perceive to be a voluntary association may be learning more about a specific subject, enlisting support for the same candidate for election to public office, fulfilling the Great Commission, improving the working conditions and employee compensation in a factory or mine, creating cooperative arrangements for the purchase and sale of farm products, coming together with other Christian believers for the corporate worship of God, or playing golf.

Whether they enlisted or were drafted or were called to active service from the National Guard or Reserve, every commissioned officer and every enlisted person in the military service of the United States during World War II was instructed repeatedly, "This is *not* a voluntary association! This is a high commitment organization that operates under a set of legal principles called the Articles of War."

A common example of this basic distinction is illustrated by organized labor. At one extreme are those employers that require a person to be a member of the appropriate labor union to be employed. Another legal principle also requires the employer to deduct the union dues from that employee's paycheck and the employee must agree to that. If the union calls a strike, every union member walks off the job.

At the other extreme is the employer with many employees. Each employee is free to join that union. If an employee does join, he or she pays those monthly dues directly to the union treasurer. If the union calls a strike, those who wish to do so walk off the job while other employees cross the picket line. That is a voluntary association of like-minded people on each side of the picket.

The Rights of the Dissenter

The rule book of the typical voluntary association usually is based on the principle of majority rule. The current majority has the authority to write, amend, and interpret the rules. By contrast, the rule book for the covenant community based on legal principles usually declares that the final authority is contained in that written constitution. Any person or organization joining it vows to accept and uphold that constitution.

Instead of following a rule book written by the current majority, that first draft of the current rule book often was written by people who have died since writing. It should be added here that in the history of civil government, constitutional democracies usually are governed by a rule book written and adopted decades earlier. When a coup d'etat brings on a dictator, one of the first steps is for that dictator to discard the old rule book and declare, "This is our new rule book. Everyone must obey my new rule book."

One avenue open to the dissenter in the voluntary organization is to organize what will become the new majority in the next election and write a new rule book. The rights of the minority can be protected by becoming the new majority.

Another way to protect the rights of the minority in the voluntary association is the right of unilateral withdrawal. For example, can that one hundred-member congregation by a vote of ninety-eight to two unilaterally decide to withdraw its membership from the denomination with which it has been affiliated for decades and take the title to the assets with it as the members decide to become an autonomous and independent congregation? Or to switch the denominational affiliation? In the voluntary association the answer is yes! In the high commitment covenant community organized on clearly defined legal principles, denominational approval is required to terminate that relationship. By definition, that right of unilateral withdrawal does not exist in the covenant community based on legal principles. That is one reason an army often is used as an analogy in describing the Christian church.

What if a member, either an individual or an organization, decides to exercise the right of unilateral withdrawal? That option is available in the voluntary association, but not in the covenant community based on legal principles. One option is to request permission to withdraw. In most American Protestant congregations the individual member may unilaterally terminate his or her membership in that congregation. In others, that termination must be approved by the governing board. This can become a source of conflict if the members perceive their congregation to be a voluntary association, but the constitution of that denomination makes it clear this is a religious body governed by legal principles. Those legal principles often require bilateral action for the withdrawal of the clergy and of congregations, but may permit unilateral withdrawal by the laity.

Another option for the dissenter is described as nullification. To understand the larger American context for that, we need to take a final detour back through the early history of this nation. On June 21, 1788, New Hampshire became the ninth state to ratify the new Constitution that would replace the Articles of Confederation. Elections were scheduled to choose the men who would staff this new system of governance. On April 30, 1789, George Washington took the oath of office as the first President to serve under this system of governance. In 1796, John Adams was elected to succeed Washington, and Adams's bitter political opponent, Thomas Jefferson, was elected to the office of Vice President. In 1798, the Federalists decided to destroy the power of the

Jeffersonian opposition by passage of the Alien Act and the Sedition Act.

In response to these two pieces of legislation, Thomas Jefferson drafted a set of resolutions declaring both acts were violations of the Constitution and were therefore null and void. These resolutions were introduced into the state legislature of Kentucky, passed, and signed by the governor. James Madison persuaded the legislature of Virginia to adopt similar legislation. Thus was born the doctrine of nullification. In a covenant community based on legal principles the dissenter can declare certain actions and laws to be null and void.

The next big chapter in this story was written by John C. Calhoun. As a revenue measure, Congress raised the tariffs on imports from abroad in 1824, 1826, and 1832. This produced economic hardships on the cotton-producing states that depended on exports. As the tariff on imports climbed, the economic attractiveness of exports declined. Vice President Calhoun wrote the statement that was adopted by the legislature of South Carolina in November 1832 as the "Ordinance of Nullification." That action nullified the legislation adopted by the United States Congress to impose the tariffs of 1828 and 1832.[2]

Subsequently Calhoun's doctrine of nullification was used to explain why the United States Congress did not possess the authority to regulate slavery in the South. Later it was used to defend the right of a state to withdraw from the union.

The Civil War of 1861–1865 was fought to defend the principle that the United States of America is *not* a voluntary association of sovereign states in which each state retains the right of withdrawal and the right to nullify the legal principles on which this covenant community is based.

If you believe your denomination resembles a covenant community based on a constitution, does that mean full-time paid officials, congregations, the clergy, midlevel judicatories, and national agencies have retained the right to ignore, disobey, or nullify the legal principles on which your denomination is based? In the nineteenth century and in the last third of the twentieth century, a common response to that question was schism.

From Vertical Systems to Horizontal Partnerships

Another big difference between those human associations organized under a set of legal principles and those organized as voluntary associations has been generated by the passage of time. As recently as the 1950s American-born adult churchgoers were comfortable with the vertical structure that governed much of life in the United States. Parents, and sometimes grandparents, controlled family life. Most of the large profit-driven corporations were governed by several layers of administrative structures. Union leaders ran the labor unions. The faculty and administration governed the colleges and universities. The 1960s brought a new demand for participatory democracy.[3] Community organizers demanded that the people who would be affected by a decision were entitled to a voice in making that decision. Most of the larger Protestant denominations in America, however, continue to rely on a representative system for governance.

The concept of horizontal partnerships is compatible with the principles of voluntary associations. These usually are voluntary relationships and often are described as cooperative arrangements. Only rarely does anyone challenge that unilateral right of withdrawal. A common example in the 1950s and 1960s was the metropolitan council of churches. In terms of governance most voluntary associations naturally seek to build a consensus in support of any important policy decision. Minority rights are protected.

In those congregations that are self-identified voluntary associations, "faithful and regular attendance in the corporate worship of God" may be a requirement for continuing as a member, but each member is allowed to define "regular." Many define it as weekly while others define it as "most Sundays" and others affirm the CEO (Christmas, Easter, and other special Occasions) definition.

Smaller human associations tend to attract people who prefer a participatory democracy as the system of governance. That helps to explain why one-half of all the Protestant congregations in the United States average fewer than 80 at worship. That also helps to explain why new missions that are averaging fewer than 60 at worship at the end of their third year rarely grow into big congregations. Those first members prefer a participatory democracy over a representative system of governance. That places a relatively low ceiling on the potential future size of that congregation.

By contrast, that large Protestant congregation organized as a high commitment covenant community and projecting high expectations of anyone seeking to become a full member usually is governed by a small number of leaders who are *not* chosen to "represent our membership." They are selected to represent what they believe is God's call to that collection of people.

If the focus is shifted to what we will describe in broad terms as denominational systems, one basic distinction is in who chooses the next generation of officials. In the Roman Catholic Church, which is designed to be a high commitment covenant community based on legal principles, headquarters chooses the leaders. Bishops are named by the Pope. Parish pastors are appointed by the bishops.

A common Protestant version calls for the regional bishop to select an assistant who eventually becomes his or her successor. When the chief executive officer of a national denominational agency departs, a department head often becomes the official successor. The governing board nominates the replacements to fill the vacancies on that board.

A middle-ground approach calls for congregations to name their delegates to the annual meeting of the regional judicatory. Those delegates subsequently elect the persons who will be voting delegates to the annual or biennial or quadrennial meeting of the legislative body governing that denomination. It is not unusual for full-time paid staff members to be selected for that role, and the governed become governors.

In those religious bodies that are organized as a voluntary association of congregations, each affiliated congregation names one or more representatives to participate in the annual or biennial policy-making deliberations of that voluntary association. Many may choose not to be directly represented.

One temptation in this discussion of the differences between those religious systems in American Protestantism that resemble voluntary associations and those that are covenant communities is to assume titles relate to performance. The high performance-covenant community usually is governed by an elite. They are not participatory democracies! That, however, does not mean that an episcopal system of church government will produce high performance while a congregational system is associated with lower level of performance. Scattered across the American ecclesiastical landscape are thousands of high expectation, high commitment, high performance congregations that are congregational in polity. One explanation for that high level of performance is they are governed by a small and often self-perpetuating elite who project high expectations and set a high bar for anyone seeking to become a full member. Another explanation for that high level of performance is the demand by both paid staff and volunteer leaders for accountability. Performance is regularly measured against challenging expectations. Frequently many of the leaders who set that high bar when the congregation was founded are still in leadership roles.

Perhaps the best illustration of this distinction came out of the discussions that led to the creation of the Protestant Episcopal Church in the United States during the last years of the eighteenth century. While it broke with a tradition that had prevailed in England since 313, the Americans decided to create an office that focused on the spiritual role of the bishop who would be elected by each state convention. The bishop retained the mitre but lost the sceptre. One scholar summarized the compromises in this sentence, "A bishop retained the spiritual functions symbolized by the mitre, but the sceptre, which symbolized the authority to rule with the aid of the state, was lost."[4]

One of the sources of misunderstanding in several Christian bodies in the United States that include the office of bishop is over the baggage carried by that title. It clearly includes spiritual leadership, but does it also carry the authority required for institutional leadership? Or does that authority have to be earned by each successor?

What Is the Central Organizing Principle?

For this discussion we will divide the congregations in American Protestantism into four categories. The largest category, in terms of congregations, is organized around three central purposes: (a) faithfully proclaim the Gospel of Jesus Christ and duly administer the sacraments, (b) transmit the Christian faith to younger generations, and (c) take care of one another. The loving shepherd, assisted by volunteers who excel in relationships, oversees what is one very large social network.

The smallest group in these four categories of congregations consists of those committed to transforming their particular religious tradition. Those who are committed to transforming their denomination, however, usually do not choose to focus on making that the central organizing principle for a congregation. Instead they are more likely to create a new protest movement or interest group that will advocate change. In recent years the two receiving the most national publicity have been movements organized to transform the Roman Catholic Church in America. One such movement is The Voice of the Faithful. Another is Survivors Network of those Abused by Priests, or SNAP. In American Protestantism these often are identified as "renewal movements."

Earlier examples in American Protestantism include movements that sought to change the stance of a particular denomination on issues such as racism, poverty, the role of women in the church, Biblical interpretation, abortion, ecumenism, the authority of the laity, human sexuality, American foreign policy, and polity.

The next smallest group of congregations include those organized to transform the world. Examples include the world missionary movement of the nineteenth century, the antislavery movement, the peace movement, the world government movement, and a variety of movements organized to alleviate world hunger.

The group with the largest number of constituents is organized around the transformation of people's lives as they accept Jesus Christ as Lord and Savior and are challenged to grow from believers into disciples and apostles. Each one of these four categories requires a different skill set in the pastor than what is appropriate for any of the other three groups.

For this discussion, the central question is, who decides which of these four approaches to ministry should guide the policy-making in a specific congregation? In that new non-denominational mission the most common answer is the founding pastor. The second most common is that first board of lay elders. In the denominationally affiliated congregations the answers vary greatly. If that denomination is organized as a high expectation, high commitment covenant community based on clearly stated legal principles, the answer almost certainly is that denomination. If, however, that denomination resembles a voluntary association, that usually means each congregation or each midlevel judicatory is free to focus on the central organizing principle its leaders prefer. Regardless of denominational affiliation in those congregations founded before 1960 and now averaging more than 500 at worship, that central organizing principle may have been chosen by the minister who now is in his or her third or fourth decade as the senior pastor of that congregation.

One of the most effective strategies for keeping the average worship attendance of any congregation, regardless of the denominational affiliation, below 100 is to focus on short pastorates of three to seven years with each new pastor introducing a central organizing principle that is different from the one followed by the immediate predecessor. An equally effective strategy for increasing the proportion of small congregations averaging fewer than 100 at worship is for the denominational policy-makers to act on the assumption this is a high commitment covenant community when most of the people responsible for implementing those policies act on the assumption this is a voluntary association. That also is an effective way to increase the intensity of intradenominational quarreling!

Donor-driven or Recipient-driven?

At this point the impatient reader may interrupt, "You've overlooked the central distinction! It's not the right of withdrawal or governance or the central organizing principle, it's money!" In recent decades that has become an important line of demarcation between the voluntary association organized around a shared commitment to a cause or need and the covenant community organized on legal principles. In both, each affiliated congregation is expected to send financial contributions to the central treasury.

In the voluntary association each congregation makes two decisions every year. The first is whether to contribute money or to terminate the relationship. The second is to decide how much money to contribute. If the goal is to collect, as a combined total for both the regional and national treasuries, an amount in excess of 3 or 4 percent of the total operating budget of each congregation—*and if the denominational policy-makers agree this is a voluntary association*—the most effective way to motivate the contributors is through designated second-mile giving. Individuals and congregations are asked to contribute to help finance the cost of specific ministries. Three that tend to have considerable appeal are planting new missions, ministries with children, and aiding the victims of a major disaster.

Given the donor-driven facet of contemporary American philanthropy, this also has become an arena of intense competition. The competitors include institutions of higher education, museums, hospitals, civic ventures, parachurch organizations, environmental groups, political candidates, world relief organizations, social justice agencies, protest movements, and a growing variety of charlatans. The Internet is competing with the offering plate. If the design calls for competing in this philanthropic arena more than once every decade or two, it is crucial to build continuing relationships with major donors and to provide full accountability on the results produced by those contributions.[5] If all the constituents, as well as the official leaders, agree their religious body is a high commitment organization based on clearly defined and universally accepted legal principles, this demand for transparency and accountability will be far less than if many of the constituents act on the assumption it really is a voluntary association.

The system for financing the budgets of most religious organizations that were created as covenant communities based on legal principles tends to continue to be recipient-driven, rather than donor-driven. One of the best-known models is the Seventh-day Adventist Church. That first tithe of a member's income is returned to the Lord via denominational channels. Congregations depend on offerings and gifts beyond that first tithe to finance their ministries. (The gap is not as great as it may first appear since that first tithe also finances the compensation of all the clergy.) The crucial point, however, is the ultimate destinations of the dollars in that first tithe are chosen by denominational officials, not by the donor.

While the details vary, that recipient-driven system of raising money also is utilized in other denominations that are self-identified covenant communities based on legal principles. Every congregation is expected to send money to finance denominational budgets. Examples include the Roman Catholic Church in America, The United Methodist Church, the Presbyterian Church (USA), and the Episcopal Church USA. The terminology varies and includes words such as appeals, assessments, apportionments, askings, taxes, and fair shares. The amount usually is stated in dollar terms and may be defined as a percentage of the congregation's operating budget or on a per capita basis or on the basis of the previous year's payments or a combination of variables. In some annual conferences in The United Methodist Church, for example, that apportionment may be adjusted upward if the congregation is experiencing numerical growth or downward if it has a shrinking membership. It may be adjusted upward if that congregation displays an excellent level of stewardship and downward if it reports a low level of stewardship. That system of rewards and punishments becomes a factor in the implementation of a turnaround strategy.

The crucial distinction, however, is the denominational system, rather than the donor, determines the ultimate destination of those charitable contributions. A typical consequence is the creation of a limited internal system of accountability that focuses on inputs, not outcomes. Congregations, for example, may be held accountable if they fail to meet their assigned quota for the number of dollars to be sent to denominational headquarters. In the extreme cases the denomination may regularly publicize each congregation's record to date in terms of the number of dollars it had been assigned to send to headquarters compared with the actual amount collected and sent. Members compare those reports with the public reports on delinquent taxes owed the county by property owners and conclude the term "tax" is the appropriate terminology for both systems.

Six Limitations

This contrast between recipient-driven and donor-driven financial contributions represents the first of a half dozen serious limitations on the usefulness of the conceptual framework described in this chapter. The most obvious is the absence of a clear and consistent line of demarcation separating those religious bodies that are primarily voluntary associations from those that were organized around that set of legal principles required to define that high commitment covenant community. The constitution of the United Church of Christ conveys the impression it is a voluntary association of autonomous congregations, conferences, associations, national agencies, and other autonomous institutions. At the other end of that spectrum is the Roman Catholic Church in America in which canon law, precedents, a highly centralized and clergy-dominated system of governance, and a variety of disciplinary procedures are combined with a conviction that the primary line of accountability is not to the current constituency, but to God. It serves as a model of the high commitment covenant community organized around a set of legal principles.

Between those two models are scores of American Protestant bodies with one foot in each camp. At this writing, for example, scores of parishes and several dioceses in the Episcopal Church USA are claiming the right to withdraw from that denomination but continue as full members of the Anglican Communion. The constitution of The United Methodist Church conveys the clear impression this is a high commitment covenant community organized around a doctrinal statement

.

and a polity that articulates the legal principles required for perpetuating that identity. Recently, however, bishops, clergypersons, congregations, and annual conferences have claimed the right of nullification. That right allows them to nullify the teachings, the accepted practices, and the law of that denomination.[6]

The current competition for the charitable dollar has encouraged leaders in the United Church of Christ, the Roman Catholic Church in America, and most other religious bodies in America to rely on both recipient-driven and donor-driven appeals to raise money.

A second and overlapping limitation is that from a national perspective several denominations appear to be organized around a set of legal principles. From a congregational perspective, however, these churches resemble a voluntary association of believers, disciples, pilgrims, inquirers, eager learners, seekers, the apathetic, birthright Christians, devoted apostles of Jesus, and spouses of believers with a relatively low threshold into membership. Most perceive their congregation to be a member of a voluntary association of congregations. No one ever challenges a member's unilateral right to withdraw. The majority of the dollars contributed by members to benevolent causes beyond that congregation's operating budget and mortgage payments do not flow through denominational channels. Most of the resources purchased to facilitate worship, learning experiences, special events, discipling, and spiritual growth were created and marketed by parachurch organizations and independent ministries rather than by their denomination.

The guiding generalization is the larger the average worship attendance and/or the faster the growth rate and/or the younger the age of recent new members, the greater the degree of disengagement from denominational agendas.

Which rule book will guide the members of the task force designing a turnaround strategy for your denomination? Will several come with the rule book for the voluntary association while others will rely on a rule book designed for high commitment covenant religious communities based on clearly defined legal principles? Or will a quarrel over which rule book to follow dominate the agenda and/or polarize the constituency?

One way to produce a variety of responses to that turn-around strategy, ranging from indifference to hostility, is for the strategy to be designed on the assumption your denomination is a covenant community while most of the congregational leaders act on the assumption it is a voluntary association.

That introduces the third limitation. How do you identify the primary constituency your congregation is seeking to reach, attract, serve, assimilate, nurture, and challenge during the next ten years? If the answer is persons born in the United States between 1840 and 1930, it may be appropriate to follow the rule book written for high commitment covenant communities with a set of clearly stated legal principles on designing or restructuring your denominational system. Build on inherited institutional loyalties and reinforce denominational loyalties. The *big* limitation on that strategy, however, is the time frame for reaching those generations is growing shorter every day.

If your goal is to reach, attract, serve, assimilate, nurture, and challenge adults born in America after 1960, you may want to discard that rule book and replace it with a new one. Instead of attempting to promote the "brand loyalty" of your denominational tradition, you may decide to accept, perhaps reluctantly, that younger generations of American church-goers resemble the rest of our consumer-driven economy. Instead of choosing a church home on the basis of denominational loyalty, they are more likely to look for a congregation that offers the relevance, quality, attractive choices, and enthusiasm they believe will nurture their own spiritual pilgrimage and that of their children.[7] Instead of looking for a congregation that loyally and faithfully seeks to obey the rules and resource the goals of its parent denomination, these younger generations are more likely to be found either in independent nondenominational congregations or in congregations in which that denomination is organized to help congregations fulfill the Great Commission. [8]

A fourth limitation of this conceptual framework reflects a long held, but perhaps naive hope of this observer. When the time comes to "Play ball!" it helps if every player is prepared to follow the same rule book. The rule book for basketball is not the same as the rule book for baseball or the one for tackle football.

If the goal is simply to design a turnaround strategy for your denomination, the easiest way to accomplish this is to use the rule book designed for high commitment covenant communities organized around a clearly stated set of legal principles. This can produce a ministry plan that states what each national denominational agency, each regional judicatory, and each of a score of different categories of congregations should do. Unfortunately that rule book does not include the instructions required to persuade every agency, judicatory, and congregation to accept and fulfill its role in implementing that comprehensive strategy.

Others may quote chapters in that rule book that explain the obligations of congregations in resourcing the attainment of denominational goals that are unrelated, and perhaps even contrary to the goals articulated in that turnaround strategy. A current example is the future of that small-town congregation that has been averaging 35 to 40 at worship since 1970. One institutional survival strategy calls for it to be served by the same minister who concurrently serves two other congregations of about the same size that also are affiliated with that same denomination. Another strategy calls for it to share a pastor with a slightly larger congregation located in or near that same small town, but affiliated with a different denomination. One church growth strategy calls for it to petition to become the "Thus and so Campus" of a very large multisite congregation. (See chapter 6.) A fourth alternative calls for it to merge with another small church. Which rule book will govern that congregation's response? The one it believes it should follow? Or the rule book used by those designing that turnaround strategy?

A fifth limitation surfaces when an American Protestant denomination that is located near the voluntary association end of this spectrum merges with a denomination that is organized around legal principles. One example of that came with the merger that produced the United Church of Christ.[9] A more recent and more complicated example is the product of several mergers over four decades that created one very large denomination out of several small-to-midsized Lutheran bodies. Those mergers created what in 1987 became the Evangelical Lutheran Church in America.

The natural institutional tendency in human associations is that as size goes up, a greater reliance is placed on legal principles. That encourages the official leadership to act on the assumption this has become a high commitment covenant community. Many of the congregational leaders, some of whom opposed one or more of those earlier mergers, are convinced the new denomination should operate as a voluntary association of congregations. One consequence may be conflict. A more passive response is what often is described as disengagement. A more serious consequence is important decisions either are not made or are made but are not implemented. Keeping a foot in each of two camps slows the pace of progress.

Finally, a sixth limitation of this conceptual framework becomes apparent when an American religious body that in contemporary practices resembles a voluntary association identifies itself as part of a global religious organization. Frequently this means bringing under one institutional umbrella self-identified voluntary association churches in America with congregations in Africa that describe their denomination as a high commitment covenant community based on clearly stated legal principles. This usually means that instead of being unifying forces, doctrine, polity, and practices become sources of conflict. The Episcopal Church

USA and The United Methodist Church are two current examples of this syndrome.

Why Chase This Rabbit?

If this conceptual framework is so difficult to explain, if it does have serious limitations, and if it can generate diversionary quarrels, why devote a whole chapter to it?

First, if all parties that will be involved in the design *and* in the implementation of that turnaround strategy agree on which rule book to follow, life will be easier for everyone and the probability of success will go up dramatically. For example, if in fact your denomination is organized and functions as a high commitment covenant community with a clearly stated set of legal principles, and if all parties agree that does represent contemporary reality and is as it should be, it will be relatively easy to design and implement a turnaround strategy. Our turnaround strategy represents the will of God. Every member, by definition, carries a responsibility to help implement it!

Likewise, if everyone agrees your denomination resembles a voluntary association of autonomous bodies (congregations, clergy, regional judicatories, national agencies, theological schools, et al.) organized to fulfill the Great Commission, the assignment of the planning committee can be expressed in eleven words—"Tell us how we can help you fulfill the Great Commission." The ultimate goal is a customized evangelistic strategy for each judicatory and for every congregation.

A variation on that would call for your planning committee to suggest two dozen options for congregations and another dozen for the midlevel judicatories. Each option could serve as a beginning point for each congregation or midlevel judicatory to design its own customized church growth strategy. The national agencies would be invited to describe the resources they can offer to congregations and judicatories. This book has been designed to provide ideas and options for these discussions.

In the real world of the mainline Protestant denominations in the United States, however, the task force assigned the responsibility to design a denominational turnaround strategy could consist of twelve individuals. Each one comes carrying a different rule book. One rule book assumes this is a high commitment covenant community with a constitution that articulates the essential legal principle. Another person carries a rule book prepared for a voluntary association of autonomous congregations, judicatories, and national agencies who have come together to promote world peace. A third rule book was designed for a voluntary association of autonomous bodies who have come together to help alleviate world hunger. A fourth rule book was designed for a voluntary association of congregations committed to fulfilling the Great Commission. A fifth was developed over the years by a voluntary association of low commitment congregations to create, operate, and fund an agency that would provide retirement benefits for the clergy. A sixth was prepared by a voluntary association of congregations to advance ecumenism. A seventh rule book was adopted more than a hundred years ago by a voluntary association of high commitment congregations to convert the heathen. The first edition of an eighth rule book was written two hundred years earlier by a voluntary association of high commitment congregations who shared the common conviction that the Roman Catholic Church was the common enemy. The contents of the remaining four rule books on that table can be described by the people who brought them.

That long paragraph introduces the second reason to chase this rabbit. Before beginning the process of designing that turnaround strategy, should the first step be to reach agreement among members of this task force on where your denomination is located on this spectrum? Is it clearly a voluntary association of autonomous congregations, judicatories, and national agencies? Or is it a high commitment covenant community with precisely stated legal principles governing those intradenominational relationships and responsibilities? Or is it somewhere between those two points on this spectrum? If so, does everyone agree on that definition of contemporary reality? Or should that perception of contemporary reality be a factor in choosing the people to serve on that task force?

The obvious reason for pursuing this discussion until agreement has been reached is in financing the implementation of your turnaround strategy. Will each congregation be assessed a fair share of the annual cost? Or will most of those dollars come in as donor-designated contributions to help finance specific components of this strategy? For example, we are living in an era when farms that have been in the same family tree for generations are now being sold to strangers. Should your denomination challenge the sellers to give a tithe from that sale to finance your strategy? Or should they give that tithe to the congregation their grandparents helped found a hundred or more years ago? Or do you send out the word, "We're looking for forty of our farm families to donate their farm for the planting of a new mission"? Who issues that challenge? The national agency responsible for new church development? A self-generated coalition of forty potential sponsor congregations? Each of several midlevel judicatories? The chief executive officer of the denomination? Who decides whether the money derived from the sale of one of those farms in Nebraska should be used to plant a new mission in California or Arizona rather than Nebraska?

A fourth and highly pragmatic reason for chasing that rabbit can be expressed in fourteen words: It's easier to go with the denominational tide than to run against that tide. In the ideal world the final version of that proposed turnaround strategy should pass this test very easily. "Is every facet of the strategy, including all phases of the implementation process, consistent with the doctrinal stance, the polity, the culture, the current priorities in the allocation of scarce resources, and the organizational structure of our denomination?"

The answer almost certainly will be, "No!" That negative response will help to pinpoint the systemic reasons for the numerical decline of your denomination during an era when church attendance in American Protestantism has been setting new records decade after decade since 1960.

From this observer's perspective it is unrealistic to expect to be able to design and implement an effective turnaround strategy without removing some of the systemic barriers to change. The one exception to that generalization is it may be possible to triple or quadruple that number of new missions planted each year without seriously challenging the status quo, but that is only one component of what should be conceptualized as a far more comprehensive strategy. For example, planting a large number of new missions that plateau in size with an average worship attendance of fewer than 150 may increase the number of small and midsized congregations in a denominational family, but that is not the most productive component of a turnaround strategy.

A fifth, and the most threatening reason to chase this rabbit, focuses on the issue of outcomes rather than inputs into that ecclesiastical system. This overlaps the issues of accountability and evaluation. The guiding generalization comes out of evaluation processes. We count what we believe is important and what we count becomes important. What does your denominational system count and regularly report? The number of nominal Christian believers whose lives were transformed as they became fully devoted followers of Jesus Christ? The number of dollars congregations send to headquarters every year? The number of baptisms? The number of new members received by profession of faith? The number of full-time career missionaries supported by your denomination? The number of votes on each side of divisive issues debated at your national denominational meetings such as American foreign policy, human sexuality, ecumenism, immigration, parental choice in the education of children, state and federal policies on taxation, subsidies to agriculture, a national energy policy, abortion, or the proposed restructure of the denominational system? The number of new missions planted each year? The proportion of new missions planted ten years ago that now average more than five hundred at worship? The number planted ten years ago that no longer exist? The number of candidates ordained each year? The annual death rate among the total membership? The number of retired clergy? The unfunded liability for retirement benefits promised the clergy? The number of full-time paid national staff positions? The number of congregations that have experienced a net increase of at least 5 percent in average worship attendance over the past five years? The number that have experienced a decrease of 5 percent or more over the past five years? The proportion of congregations that did not receive any new members by either baptism or profession of faith during the past year? The number of congregations that dissolved last year? The number that merged with another church of your denomination last year? The net increase or decrease in the number of congregations for each of the past ten years? The change in the number that averaged at least 800 at worship over the past decade? The change in the number of congregations that averaged 500 or more at worship in 1990, and how many of those that averaged 500 or more in 1990 now average fewer than 350? The number of times the chief executive officer of each regional judicatory has been arrested for civil disobedience? The number of congregations that had been worshiping at the same address for at least twenty years before relocating their meeting place between 1981 and 2000 that (a) have at least doubled their average worship attendance or (b) have experienced a decrease of at least 20 percent or more in their average worship attendance since relocation?

When those and similar reports are published each year, what is the response? To ignore them since "We focus on quality, not quantity"? To attempt to identify and name the culprits that have produced the bad news? To sort out the positive reports and celebrate those victories? Or to ask three questions? (1) Are those the outcomes we want our system to produce? (2) If not, why are the desired outcomes not being produced by our system? (3) Is it possible that we desire outcomes our system is not designed to produce?

One example is the denominational system that was designed many decades ago to be a high expectation, high commitment covenant community based on precisely defined legal principles to reach, attract, serve, nurture, assimilate, and challenge the generations born before 1920. During the past half century that denomination had drifted in the direction of becoming a voluntary association. One problem is the changes required to function as a voluntary association have not been made in the system of governance nor in the expectations projected of congregations. A second is the shrinking number of American churchgoers born before 1920. Drift and death have eroded the vitality and relevance of that denomination.

A second example is the denomination that, through a series of mergers since the Civil War, has transformed what once were five or six or more different religious traditions into one. One or two of the predecessors were clearly voluntary associations while one or two resembled high commitment covenant communities based on clearly defined legal principles. For at least one or two others that was not an issue. They were a collection of worshiping communities united around a common religious heritage, a common language, a common culture, a common ancestry, and the concerns common among venturesome people who had left the old country to carve out a new life in the new world. Two or three generations later, mergers produced two or three new denominations. Institutional survival, transmitting the faith to younger generations, creating new institutions such as homes, hospitals, colleges, seminaries, and missions became the unifying principles. They also became the basis for institutional self-evaluation. Deaths, births, the shortage of new immigrants from that same "old country," and urbanization changed the constituency. The call for efficiency, economy, and the desire to reduce what had become an obsolete institution filled with redundancy motivated the call for more mergers. Mergers require compromises. Should this new denomination be designed to be a high commitment covenant community or a voluntary association? An attractive compromise was, "We'll combine the best of each of our traditions in creating this new denomination and minimize quarrels over structure, by not writing a new rule book."

A decade later a crucial question remains unanswered. Should we design a system for that annual audit of performance that is compatible with a voluntary association of congregations, judicatories, national agencies, and other institutions or should it be a system that is compatible with the high expectation, high commitment covenant community based on clearly defined principles?

An attractive alternative has turned out to be, "We have two goals. One is to keep everyone happy. The second is to keep the money flowing into headquarters." Among the normal and predictable consequences of that decision are disengagement, quarrels over money, intradenominational conflicts over values and goals, finger-pointing, and an erosion of inherited denominational loyalties and the struggle for control by caucuses and other interest groups.

One price tag is increased difficulty in designing and implementing a turnaround strategy in a denomination that has yet to decide on its own identity.

CHAPTER THREE

DESIGNING A
TURNAROUND STRATEGY

If we know what to do to reach large numbers of
Americans born after 1960 and recent immigrants and we
also know how to do it, why are so many Protestant
denominations reporting an aging and shrinking of their constituencies? One answer was the theme of the first chapter.
Many of the denominational systems that produced desirable
outcomes in the 1950s have become obsolete. New ways of
farming, of selling groceries, of mining coal and iron ore, of
transporting people from Point A to Point B, of raising
money, of communicating information, and of reaching
people with the Gospel of Jesus Christ have replaced the old
systems.

The old systems that produced the desired outcomes in the
1950s no longer are competitive. Can new systems be
designed to produce the desired outcomes? Can a turnaround
strategy be designed and implemented to reach younger
generations?

Those questions introduce one of the most critical questions in this entire process. What will be the first step? One
alternative could be to select the people who will design a
turnaround strategy. What are the criteria to be used in identifying these people? Will the turnaround strategy be

designed by one group while the responsibility for implementing it will be placed on those who were not involved in designing it? Or will those responsible for the implementation be represented among the active participants in designing it? Will the leaders, both clergy and lay, from those congregations that have been most effective in reaching, attracting, serving, nurturing, assimilating, and challenging younger generations dominate the designing process? What will be the criteria used in choosing those assigned the responsibility to design this turnaround strategy?

What Is the Assignment?

The other alternative begins by describing the assignment. Instead of choosing the task force and giving them a blank sheet of paper on which to write the strategy, this option begins with describing the assignment. That makes it easier to articulate the criteria required to select the appropriate people for filling that assignment. The relevance of making this the first step can be illustrated by seven different models.

The first is the blank sheet of paper planning model. If your denomination did not have any affiliated congregations in this region, what would be the ideal design for mission and ministry in the twenty-first century? Would it call for a network of congregations composed largely of constituents who trace most or all of their ancestry back to Western Europe? Or would it call for a collection of monocultural congregations with many serving a predominantly Anglo constituency, while others served Koreans and Korean Americans, a substantial number worshiped in Spanish, another group were for Latinos comfortable in English, another group of congregations were designed for American-born blacks, a couple were designed for recent immigrants from India, several were either self-identified Afrocentric churches or African American congregations, and one or two worshiped in Mandarin?

Would that design for the future call for geographically defined multicultural regional judicatories composed of monocultural congregations? Or would it be designed with nongeographical monocultural affinity midlevel judicatories?

In other words, this option calls for designing the future first. A subsequent step would be to design a plan that would transform today's reality into that vision for tomorrow. This planning model has been used in recent decades in America to transform retail trade, the delivery of health care services, the structure of financial institutions, and public education for ages five to eighteen.

Instead of using ethnicity as the primary line of demarcation in identifying future constituents, a second planning model uses theological stance. Since the words "liberal" and "conservative" both carry too much diversionary baggage, we will use two terms that have been around for many decades. Those who turn first to Scripture to define their theology are identified as residents of Jerusalem. Those who choose to test every doctrinal statement against human reason and personal experience are described as residents of Athens.[1]

Does your ministry plan for the year 2025 call for reaching migrants to this community from Athens? Or migrants from Jerusalem? Or both? If both, does that mean you expect every congregation will be able to accommodate both Athenians and Jerusalemites? Or do you plan for each community in which your denomination will be represented to be served by at least two congregations—one for people educated in Athens and one for those reared in Jerusalem?

Can one congregation serve both constituencies? The historical record is clearly in the affirmative! The largest number are smaller congregations in which the number one source of internal cohesion is ancestry and language or skin color, and the number two source of cohesion is kinship ties. Typically the third cohesive force is that most of the people have built their primary personal social network from members of this congregation. Frequently those social ties are reinforced by the members sharing a meal together at least a dozen times every year.

A second example of the theologically pluralistic church is the large congregation led by a long-tenured senior pastor who displays the magnetic personality that enables hundreds of members to explain, "Our pastor is one of my four or five closest personal friends." That relationship may be reinforced by skin color or language or social class or place of birth or upward mobility or the identification of a common enemy or therapeutic preaching or direct support of one or more church-related social welfare institutions or a Christian day school.

Does your ministry plan for 2025 begin with a blank sheet of paper? Or does it focus on migrants from Jerusalem or on migrants from Athens?

A third, radically different planning model also begins with a vision of a new tomorrow. This vision calls for this judicatory to consist of a collection of high expectation, high commitment covenant communities. Each congregation will be designed with a high threshold into membership and a low threshold at the exit door. From a denominational perspective this will be an expression of the high expectation, high commitment covenant community built on a foundation of clearly defined legal principles and a doctrinal statement marked by clarity and certainty. There would be a notable absence of ambiguity! This model is widely used in American Protestantism today. It attracts both people from Jerusalem and the disenchanted migrants who had been educated in Athens. It usually produces an annual denominational report in which the average worship attendance exceeds the total reported membership.

A subsequent step in this third model calls for designing a plan to (a) transform what are low commitment and midlevel commitment congregations into high commitment churches and (b) plan new missions designed to be high expectation, high commitment worshiping communities from day one.

A fourth planning model for a new tomorrow is based on the assumption that the privately owned motor vehicle is here to stay and that large regional institutions are replacing neighborhood institutions. If, for example, your region includes thirty cities that range in population from 10,000 to more than 100,000, one long-term goal could be that each of these thirty cities would include one or more very large regional congregations averaging at least 800 to 1,000 in weekend worship attendance. That usually requires a meeting place with somewhere between 10 and 200 acres of usable land plus modern physical facilities. Among the first questions to be asked in designing this scenario are these five:

1. Which of our currently affiliated congregations represents this model? Could it serve as a teaching church to help propagate this model?
2. Which of our affiliated congregations has both the potential and the eagerness to accept this role? What will each one require in order to complete the transformation?
3. Where should we be planting new missions designed to become very large regional churches?
4. In reflecting on these three questions, which should be the first priority? The second? The third priority?
5. What other components should be included in our turnaround strategy?

The fifth planning model begins by reviewing that five-year audit of recent performance. That audit could reveal that (a) 42 percent of our congregations reported a decrease in average worship attendance, (b) nearly one-half reported they have lost more members than they received, (c) two-thirds of the new missions we planted during the previous five years either have plateaued in size with an average worship attendance under 100 or no longer exist, (d) the total number of affiliated congregations decreased by 9 percent, and (e) the median age of our confirmed membership increased by nearly two years.

The assignment is to design a turnaround strategy that will produce more desirable outcomes. That assignment could lead your task force to produce a twelve-point report resembling these recommendations:

1. Revitalize aging and numerically shrinking congregations.
2. Plant more new missions.
3. Provide better continuing education experiences for pastors in evangelism.
4. Increase the enrollment of American-born blacks and Latinos in our seminaries.
5. Endow a chair in evangelism in every seminary.
6. Encourage more of our very small churches to merge.
7. Encourage congregations meeting in obsolete facilities on an inadequate site at what has become a poor location to relocate.
8. Expand our Sunday schools.
9. Strengthen our ministries with teenagers.
10. Encourage smaller congregations in sparsely populated rural communities to enter into ecumenical partnerships and share a pastor with a nearby church.
11. Require every congregation to have an active committee on evangelism.
12. Launch a capital funds campaign to finance the implementation of this strategy.

Our sixth planning model begins with that identical five-year audit of performance, but carries a different assignment. Systems produce the outcomes they are designed to produce. We are dissatisfied with the outcomes our system has been producing. The assignment for this task force consists of two parts. First, identify and describe the desired outcomes our system can and should be producing. Second, identify the changes that must be made in our system to enable it to produce the desired outcomes.

If this becomes the assignment, one of the two or three top criteria in selecting members of the task force will be competence in the use of systems theory in planning. If the denominational system has become dysfunctional, it is unrealistic to expect that either exhortation or more money will produce desired outcomes. Systemic changes will be required to produce those desired outcomes. (See the last five pages of chapter 7 for this model.)

The last of these seven planning models offered here to illustrate the variations in assignments may be the most widely used. The first step in the process of designing a turnaround strategy is to select the members of that task force. The second step is to give them their assignment. While stated in more polite language, this is a summary of that assignment:

"We're facing a crisis. We are experiencing decreases in membership, in worship attendance, and in the number of congregations. Our members are growing older, the death rate among our confirmed members continues to rise, and most of our churches are not able to attract younger generations. Your assignment is to design a turnaround strategy that will win broad-based support and not polarize our constituency."

In other words, "Let's play the cards we've been dealt and produce a strategy that will turn a losing hand into a winning hand."

What Are the Criteria?

The point of describing these seven different planning models is to support the contention that the assignment should be clearly defined before any attempt is made to agree on the criteria for selecting the members of the task force who will be asked to carry out that assignment. If, for example, a top priority is to transform a predominantly Anglo denomination into a multicultural religious body, the criteria will not be the same as would be appropriate if the goal is to redesign what has become a dysfunctional system. Likewise, if the goal is to increase the number of regional megachurches, that will require selecting people who have had extensive experience as congregational leaders in that type of congregation.

Where Do Americans Go to Church?

After defining the assignment to be given to this task force and agreeing on the criteria to be used in selecting the members, the agenda can be shifted to focus on a third question. Where do Americans go to church in these early years of the twenty-first century? In 1955, ancestry, skin color, language, geographical proximity, inherited denominational loyalties, kinship ties, and the religious affiliation of one's spouse were highly influential. Skin color and language continue to be powerful determinants today, but for churchgoers whose ancestors came from Western Europe, ancestry is less influential.

Where do American Protestants go to church today? That is a book-length subject, but five patterns stand out that are relevant to this discussion. First, and most obvious, a disproportionately large number are worshiping with congregations that either (a) were founded since 1960 or (b) moved to their current meeting place after 1960. They are either relatively new missions or they have relocated to write a new chapter in their history. These younger generations prefer to help create the new rather than to perpetuate the old.

Second, a disproportionately large number can be found in very large churches. The largest 1 percent of all the Protestant congregations in America account for approximately 14 percent of all Protestant worshipers on the typical weekend and the largest 5 percent of churches account for close to 25 percent of worshipers, the same as the smallest 60 percent of churches. The remaining 35 percent of churches account for the other half.

Third, the definition of "large" is changing. In 1985, for example, the very largest Protestant congregations in America averaged between 8,000 and 17,000 at worship. Today that bracket is 15,000 to 25,000 at weekend worship. The United Methodist Church, for example, is a predominantly small-church denomination in which one-half of all congregations report an average worship attendance of 53 or fewer. In 1987 the ten largest congregations ranged in size with an average worship attendance between 1,758 and 3,235. Fifteen years later the ten largest averaged somewhere between 2,895 and 7,100 in reported worship attendance. The second largest congregation in 1987 reported 2,845. That would have been good for eleventh place in 2002.

Fourth, a disproportionately large number of the very largest Protestant congregations in the United States are benefiting from the leadership of a long-tenured senior minister, who often is the founding pastor.

Fifth, and perhaps most significant, fewer churchgoers are walking to church than in 1960 and more of those who drive are traveling six to thirty-five miles each way. That contrasts with the service area with a radius of less than six miles in 1960.

The Criteria for Setting Priorities

A crucial and often divisive issue for that special task force requires early deliberation. What are the criteria that will be used to determine the priorities in what is hoped to be a productive turnaround strategy?

Given the limited resources of every regional judicatory or denominational system, which components of a larger strategy are most likely to produce the greatest returns on an investment of those scarce resources? Therefore the first criterion in determining the rank order of the components discussed in this chapter is productivity. Which ones are most likely to be effective? The second criterion is difficulty. The approaches that tend to be most difficult are placed at or near the end of this chapter. The ones that are relatively easy to implement are discussed first. These two criteria result in moving new church development down the list and the revitalization of aging congregations to near the end. They also move encouraging long pastorates up to near the top.

A useful guiding generalization is that while long pastorates do not necessarily produce numerically growing congregations, it is rare to find a congregation that has enjoyed years of sustained numerical growth without the benefit of a long pastorate. Therefore long pastorates should be a high priority if the goal is to reach, attract, serve, assimilate, nurture, and challenge substantial numbers of newcomers year after year.

The driving generalization is the larger the size of the congregation and/or the larger the number of newcomers each year and/or the greater the number of worship experiences offered each weekend and/or the younger the constituency and/or the larger the proportion of constituents who are third- or fourth- or fifth-generation American-born residents and/or the weaker the denominational ties and/or the greater the emphasis on welcoming strangers and/or the weaker the influence of skin color or national ancestry and/or the lower the level of religious commitment among the members and/or the weaker the power of kinship ties and/or the shorter the period of time this congregation has been worshiping in this same room and/or the greater the degree of demographic diversity among the constituents and/or the greater the variety of previous religious allegiances of the current constituents and/or the greater the emphasis in the corporate worship of God on the Word rather than the liturgy or the sacraments, the greater the degree of continuity that is lodged in the ministerial staff in general and the senior minister in particular.

The other version of that long sentence is one of the most effective tactics in reducing the size of midsized and large Protestant congregations is to encourage short pastorates of two to ten years.

What produces long pastorates in numerically growing congregations? This traveler's experiences suggest three of the crucial variables recur over and over again. First, this is a good match between the needs of this congregation at this point in its history and the gifts, skills, personality, passion, priorities, theological stance, experience, age, and vocational goals of that minister. Second, if that pastor is married, the spouse is happy to be married to a parish pastor, is pleased to be married to the pastor of this particular congregation, is comfortable living in this community, and is content with the expectations people project of "our Pastor's spouse."

Third, that pastor is a self-motivated lifelong learner who is both able and eager to master the new skills required as that congregation not only grows in numbers, but also redefines its identity role and priorities.[2]

I. and II. The Top Two Components

Those six paragraphs introduce what this pilgrim believes should be at the top of the list when the time comes to design a denominational turnaround strategy.

The first is to adopt a ministerial placement system designed to produce good matches between congregation and pastor. This is a far more demanding challenge today than it was fifty years ago! The differences among generations, among institutions in general (commercial airlines, hospitals, motion picture theaters, manufacturers of motor vehicles, grocery stores, motels, financial institutions, public high schools, and Protestant congregations) and among members of any one generation including Christian ministers, are far greater today than they were in the 1950s. The demand today is for a customized match.

This often means turning to a national, rather than a regional inventory, in searching for the successor to the departing pastor. Thanks to relatively low cost airfares and to modern technology (videotapes, conference telephone calls, video conferences, and the Internet), this can be a relatively inexpensive process.

A rapidly growing number of congregations also are recognizing the value of specialized competence and experience in producing good matches. That person may be a denominational staff member who specializes in placement. It may be an independent parish consultant. It may be a parachurch organization that specializes in national searches. It may be a seven-person call committee with four or five of the members chosen for their professional skill and experience in managing human resources.

For some denominational leaders the most disturbing consequence arises out of the fact that today the differences within a denominational family often are greater than the differences between the two denominations. One result is the Southern Baptist minister is invited to serve as the new pastor of what becomes a rapidly growing United Methodist congregation in Texas or a Presbyterian minister in Pennsylvania becomes the new pastor of a United Church of Christ congregation in the Midwest or a Lutheran pastor in Indiana organizes a new independent church in Illinois or a minister from an independent megachurch becomes the new senior pastor of a denominationally affiliated congregation on the West Coast.

On a cost-benefit basis, creating and maintaining a ministerial placement system designed to produce good matches ranks at the top of this list of components for a denominational turnaround strategy. Close behind it is the related goal of long pastorates. Given the fact that not every congregation wants to double or quadruple in size and that many ministers prefer to move to a new challenge every few years, a reasonable goal is not to attempt to replicate the Congregational Church's model of colonial times of pastorates of twenty years or more.[3] One reason, of course, is today pastorates are far more likely to be terminated by retirement rather than by death as was the pattern in the eighteenth century. A second is upward mobility is a more common goal today.

Therefore, a reasonable goal could be that in 15 percent of the congregations the typical pastorate exceeds thirty years while in another 35 percent it is between fifteen and thirty years. That would produce a median tenure of fifteen years. One consequence would be that when the forty-six-year-old pastor in Texas is invited to become a candidate for the position of senior minister of a large congregation in Ohio, the reply would be, "I'm flattered to be asked, but I can't consider a move since I've only been in this church twelve years. It would be premature for me to consider moving."

III. Identify the Primary New Constituency

A popular slogan among American Protestant congregations is, "We welcome everyone." That, of course, it not an accurate representation of reality. Among those who probably would not feel welcome are the people who are not comfortable worshiping God in English, those in wheelchairs, those who are deaf or blind, and those who do not see anyone in the building who resembles them in age or skin color or in the way they are dressed. One reason we affirm the existence of other Christian churches in the community is because we recognize no one congregation can serve everyone. Only a few pastors, for example, are fluent in ten or fifteen languages.

Likewise, if any one Protestant denomination in the United States possessed both the resources and the commitment required to serve a demographically diverse and theologically pluralistic constituency, it would either be the fastest growing religious body in the nation or the one with the highest level of intradenominational quarreling. The pragmatic compromise is similar to the one at the drugstore on Main Street. "We welcome anyone and everyone who would like to come in and purchase any of the items we stock. If you need a new pair of shoes or a set of new tires for your car, however, we don't stock those. You'll have to go elsewhere for that need to be filled."

The point of those two paragraphs is no one of America's many denominational systems has the resources required to respond in a relevant and effective manner to the religious needs of every resident of this country. That is one explanation for the long discussion of the assignment earlier in this chapter. This point can be illustrated by a brief look at ten categories of the American population. As you design a turnaround strategy for your denomination, which of these do you expect will account for at least 40 percent of the people who will join a congregation affiliated with your denomination during the next five years?

1. One large group consists of those who believe the top priority is to transmit the Christian faith to the children and grandchildren of the current membership in a manner that also will instill in them a strong denominational loyalty. One way the Church of Jesus Christ of Latter-day Saints does this is to expect every young adult will devote one and one-half or two years of his or her life to full-time volunteer missionary service. One way to strengthen one's faith and reinforce one's denominational loyalty is to spend every day for a year or two articulating that faith to others.

2. The primary constituency for our evangelistic efforts consists of self-identified happy atheists and contented agnostics who are *not* on a religious quest. This is the category in which you will encounter little effective competition.

3. The primary constituency consists of believers on a spiritual search for meaning in life. They are looking for a "church that embodies promise and purpose amid the world's doubts and struggles."

4. Overlapping that is another very large group. These are self-identified Christian believers who are looking for a church that proclaims the Gospel of Jesus Christ in a message filled with certainty, clarity, and hope. They are weary of

ambiguity. They are bored by preachers who score lower than a grade of A+ on communication skills.[4] Many have given up on finding such a church. Others continue to drift from congregation to congregation as they shop for their dream to be fulfilled. The new mission that is able to deliver what these searchers are seeking often becomes a megachurch before its fifth birthday.

5. A related group is looking for a church home that offers and has the resources to fulfill a two-part promise. "We're here to help you rear your children and we're here to help you transmit the Christian faith to your children." Many of these are organized around (a) worship, (b) a Christian day school that is the heart of a package of ministries designed for parents with young children, (c) an attractive package of ministries designed for parents of teenagers and (d) meaningful ministries with teenagers, usually staffed largely by adult volunteers who are models of a deeply committed Christian and who accept the role of mentors. The recent surge of interest in religion among Americans born after 1985 is one explanation for the rapid growth of hundreds of contemporary megachurches.

6. A completely different focus is on reaching and attracting migrants from other religions including "cradle Catholics," Jews, Muslims, and Buddists.

7. Close to that are those churches that seek to reach and welcome married couples who were reared in two different religious traditions. The Lutheran marries a Baptist. They agree their new church home will be something other than Lutheran or Baptist. As recently as the 1950s one reason parents sent their eighteen-year-olds to a denominationally affiliated college was to increase the probability that the Lutheran would meet and marry a Lutheran while the Presbyterian would meet and marry a Presbyterian, and the Methodist would meet and marry a Methodist. Today people tend to marry later in life. As a result they are more likely to meet their future spouse in the workplace or at a social event or in a recreation league or in a coffee shop or at Home Depot ®.

8. High on the list of prospective future constituents in many congregations are the newcomers to that community who are in search of a new church home. In the 1950s it was easier to locate that constituency in a new residential subdivision. Today that is about the fifth best place to look. Word of mouth recommendations, direct mail, the Internet, and huge events (such as on Good Friday or Easter Saturday or Christmas Eve) rank ahead of close geographical proximity in attracting new residents.

9. While this is a highly subjective issue and complicated by varying definitions of key words, it appears the 1950s saw younger generations leaving the fundamentalist traditions for theologically more liberal churches if and when they switched their congregational allegiances. Today it appears the generations born after 1960 are more likely to seek an evangelical church if and when they switch their congregational affiliation. The migration to the left has been replaced by a migration to the center.[5] When they look for a church home, these younger generations tend to prefer a congregation populated by adults reared in Jerusalem (the city of faith) rather than Athens (the city of reason). (This identifies a crucial criterion in selecting members for the task force to design a turnaround strategy. Will the planning be dominated by people from Athens or from Jerusalem?)

10. One of the most interesting patterns is reflected among many Americans who (a) were born before 1940, (b) recently changed their place of residence, (c) no longer have the skills to meet and make new friends they displayed three or four decades earlier, (d) have watched their old social network shrink due to retirements, deaths, and relocations, and (e) enjoy good physical and mental health.

One appeal is to challenge these mature adults to be engaged in doing ministry in intergenerational settings such as building or remodeling a house for Habitat for Humanity or signing up to be a short-term volunteer missionary for a week or two every year with a team going to work in ministry with fellow Christians in a sister church on another continent or volunteering to staff a ministry to feed the hungry or to shelter the homeless or to tutor children. A common outcome is summarized in that ancient bit of wisdom, "You know you belong when you know you're needed." One fringe benefit is "doing good." Another is meeting and making new friends.

In other congregations the staffing of off-campus ministries in that multisite church, the expansion of the ministry of music, or overnight and three- or four-day bus trips to interesting destinations are channels for reaching this slice of the adult population.

If it is encouraged, these ministries also can be a valuable component of a strategy in what has always been an all-Anglo congregation to attract, welcome, and assimilate adults from other racial and ethnic groups.

It would be easy to refine and expand that list to fifty categories, but ten illustrate why this should be high on the priority list of components for anyone responsible for designing a church growth strategy for a congregation or a regional judicatory. Which slice of the population are you seeking to reach, attract, serve, nurture, assimilate, and challenge? What resources will be required to do that? On a larger scale those same two questions are relevant to those designing a denominational turnaround strategy. One big difference is the most effective congregational strategies tend to focus on "people who are like us." By contrast, a denominational turnaround strategy may place a high priority on attracting people "who are not like us" or "who are younger than our present constituency."

IV. Replace Factionalism and Intradenominational Quarreling with a Unifying Vision of One Clearly Defined Role for Your Denomination

Currently the internal quarreling in several American Protestant denominations has produced divisive adversarial relationships. This can be seen in both scores of regional judicatories as well as between congregations and the national denominational leadership. Among the other outcomes are litigation and the disengagement of congregational leaders who have concluded, "We don't have a dog in that fight." The most serious outcome, of course, has been the diversion of time, energy, creativity, money, and other resources from evangelism and missions.

In at least three or four of the larger Protestant denominations the level of internal quarreling has reached the point that the most practical alternative may be schism. A simpler but far less popular alternative is to open the safety valve by encouraging the most discontented congregations to disaffiliate and take an unrestricted title to their assets with them as they depart. That option has been utilized by Lutherans, Presbyterians, and others in recent decades.

If a denomination is becoming increasingly polarized over doctrine and/or polity and the differences appear to be irreconcilable, dividing into two or three denominations may be the most promising road back to making fulfillment of the Great Commission the top priority.

American Presbyterians, who often are a couple of decades ahead of other denominations in responding to new developments, have modeled schism as a strategy for reducing the level of internal quarreling. That option is on the table for Southern Baptists, Episcopalians, United Methodists, the Evangelical Lutheran Church in America, and others.

A persuasive argument can be made that achieving agreement on a unifying denominational vision is so central to any turnaround strategy that it should be placed first, rather than fourth, in this chapter. One explanation is the apparent lack of interest in making this the top priority. A second is the absence of agreement on the identity of the person or agency who combines the creativity, responsibility, authority, and courage with the support required to cast that vision. A third explanation is found in the calendar. How much time will be required to accomplish this? The thirty-seven-year-old may decide, "Given my life expectancy, I cannot expect to see this goal attained in my lifetime, so let's ignore it." How much time is left before that growing number of fires consumes all the resources?

A fourth explanation for not making this a high priority goes back to the discussion in the previous chapter. Should our denomination act like a voluntary association or a high commitment religious body? Many of today's church shoppers reply, "I have zero interest in reforming any denomination! I'm looking for a church that focuses on the spiritual growth of people like me."

A fifth reason for not making this a high priority is purely pragmatic. While the policy-makers attempt to achieve agreement on the theme of that unifying denominational vision and on the contents of the strategy required to turn that vision into reality, the numerical decline continues. The median age of the constituency continues to climb. A three-part compromise could consist of (a) the policy-makers focusing on the formulation of that unifying vision, (b) outsourcing to parachurch organizations assistance for congregations searching for a new pastor to find that ideal match, and (c) enlisting leaders from the very largest congregations in that denomination to design and begin to implement the strategy to increase the number of very large churches.

Depending on the polity and the degree of internal harmony within your denomination as a whole as well as in each regional judicatory, concurrent efforts could be undertaken by various task forces to implement one or more of the remaining components of a turnaround strategy.

Finally, another pragmatic reason for placing a very low priority on formulating that unifying denominational vision is it may be too late to include that in a turnaround strategy. In at least four or five of the largest Christian religious bodies in the United States—and that list may include the Roman Catholic Church in America—the chasms that now separate the various factions are so wide and so deep they cannot be bridged with a simple unifying vision. The more comprehensive that vision and the more precisely defined the operational strategy required for implementation, the more likely it will lead to schism rather than to a turnaround. Thus those readers committed to turning around their denomination's numerical decline and opposed to schism may prefer to drop this suggestion from fourth to nineteenth place in designing an eighteen-point customized turnaround strategy for their denomination.

V. The Staff Configuration

Why do so many of the large Protestant congregations that average between six hundred and eight hundred plateau in size rather than continue to grow in numbers? The highly visible explanation for many of them is a shortage of space and especially the shortage of off-street parking.

Less visible, but often more influential, are several other differences. In nine out of ten of the predominantly Anglo Protestant congregations in the United States, lay volunteers usually have a highly influential voice in making decisions on schedules, the creation of new ministries, staffing, the design of construction programs, the operation of the ministry of education, the allocation of dollars for mission needs, and the design of the worship experiences. In the very large congregations most of these and similar decisions are made, or at least initiated, by paid staff. The larger the size of the congregation, the larger the proportion of lay volunteers engaged in doing ministry rather than administration.

A related big difference is the larger the size of the congregation, the larger the proportion of program staff who are specialists rather than generalists. That long list includes Minister of Missions, Executive Pastor, Director of the Early Childhood Development Center, Parish Nurse, Program Director, Media Specialist, Minister of Congregational Life, Youth Team Leader, Director of Learning Communities, Senior Ministries Director, and Worship Leader. One consequence is the larger the size of the congregation, the larger the proportion of paid program staff who are lay rather than clergy, part-time rather than full-time, and female rather than male. By contrast, the vast majority of the full-time paid program staff in congregations averaging 85 to 125 at worship are ordained males. In addition, the larger the size of the congregation, the greater the probability the program staff will be organized as teams with a substantial number of part-time paid laypersons plus lay volunteers.

Why do so many congregations averaging 135 to 350 at weekend worship plateau in size rather than double or triple in numbers? Three of the most common explanations are (a) a shortage of space, (b) a refusal by the senior minister to accept the need to redefine "my role, my responsibilities, and our primary constituency," and (c) a refusal to redesign the staff configuration.

Those reflections explain why helping larger congregations redesign their staff configuration earns a high priority in designing a turnaround strategy for a Protestant denomination in contemporary America.

Another example of this same issue consists of the 100,000 American Protestant congregations averaging 65 to 135 at worship. Many of these have the potential to double or triple in size during the next decade. Frequently, however, the staff configuration is organized around the pastor who is a loving shepherd rather than a visionary and evangelistic leader. If, when the time comes to search for a successor for that departing loving shepherd, the congregation can be persuaded to a change in the criteria for selecting a successor, that can be a productive component of that larger strategy.

VI. The Fragile Nature of Very Large Congregations

The importance of the staff configuration introduces a sixth component for that denominational strategy. What happened to those very large Protestant congregations that were averaging 800 or more at worship back in 1960? This observer's sample of that universe has revealed that more than one-half had experienced a decrease of at least 35 percent in average worship attendance by the end of the twentieth century. Why did that happen? In only a tiny percentage of the churches studied could a decline in the total population in the community be identified as the cause for that decline in attendance. The seven most frequently identified factors did not include a decrease in population. While these were the seven most frequent factors, the impact of each one varied greatly from one very large congregation to the next. In general, however, they could be ranked in this order of influence.

1. A failure back in the 1960s or 1970s or early 1980s to develop a new ministry plan designed for a new role and to reach or serve a new constituency. The temptation was to believe "the road that brought us to today is the road that will take us to tomorrow." Too often that attractive road of the 1960s and 1970s terminated in a dead end in the 1980s or 1990s.

One example of a dead end was the role of the largest congregation of a denomination in a particular county in 1960. A denominational merger redefined that to being the third largest church of the new denomination in this county. A second example was the role as "the college church" or "university church" attracted students, faculty, and administrative staff in the 1950s, but the proliferation of parachurch ministries on the campus in the 1960s and 1970s eroded that role. A third example was Old First Church Downtown that attracted the shakers and movers of the secular community in the middle third of the twentieth century but failed to attract their successors. A fourth example was the new suburban mission founded after World War II as a neighborhood church that grew rapidly. By 1975 or 1980, however, it was limited by a functionally obsolete building on a site with severely limited off-street parking. What worked for the neighborhood church was not appropriate for the role of a large regional congregation.

2. The staff configuration designed for that 1965 role was not appropriate for that new role. When a staff member departed, the temptation was to fill the vacancy rather than to redefine the position or, better yet, staff a new ministry plan.

3. The successor to that long-tenured senior minister turned out to be a mismatch in terms of gifts, skills, et al. In addition, the departing senior minister often had seniority on 70 to 100 percent of the members. The successor came in at the bottom of the seniority ladder. The predecessor had shaped the culture and set the priorities. The successor inherited that culture and also inherited someone else's priorities.

A common pattern was that long-tenured senior pastor was followed by a two-year unintentional interim minister, who was followed by the five-year pastorate of a minister who brought a different set of priorities, who was followed by a six-year ministry by a senior pastor who sought to reform the congregational culture or completely replace the inherited staff or introduce a new set of priorities or advocate a substantially different theological perspective. As a result of those three pastorates, in twelve to fifteen years the worship attendance had dropped to one-third to one-half of the peak back in "the good old days of Doctor Harrison."

The first guiding generalization is the larger the constituency of that nonprofit institution, the more central is the role of the official leader. Examples include mayor, governor, President of the United States, high school principal, foundation chief executive, university president or chancellor, and senior minister.

The second guiding generalization is the weaker the denominational loyalty and/or the faster the rate of numerical growth and/or the shorter the tenure of the most influential lay volunteer leaders and/or the more extensive and complex the schedule and/or the younger the age of recent new members and/or the more extensive the off-campus ministries, the more likely the continuity is in the person and personality of that senior minister.

4. Demographic changes in the population living within the area served by that congregation created new challenges. The obvious ones were a change in the skin color or ancestry or language or culture or social class of the newcomers.

Equally serious, but without the same high visibility, was the impact of the demographic change that saw a population of upper middle class and American-born residents of Western European ancestry born before 1940 replaced by new generations of upper middle class and American-born residents of Western European ancestry born after 1960. Frequently these younger generations brought a different set of values, characteristics, and expectations than did those older residents. These younger generations displayed a lower degree of denominational loyalty; they preferred to help pioneer the new rather than perpetuate the old; they preferred horizontal partnerships to vertical lines of authority; they found it relatively easy to commute ten or more miles to work, to shop, to recreation, to entertainment, and to church; they placed a higher value on quality; they demanded choices; they expected to find a vacant parking space at a convenient location at the end of their journey; as a group, they expected the church would nurture their spiritual pilgrimage; they assumed the church should operate on a seven-day-a-week schedule in order to offer them a broader range of choices; and many expected the church existed to help them rear their children.

5. Perhaps most significant, those older generations had been socialized into a producer-driven economy. Their younger successors have been socialized by a consumer-driven culture. That changed the name of the game. Many of what in the 1960s or 1970s had been very large congregations had thrived in a religious culture that rewarded great preaching, great music, and an extensive Sunday school. By the 1990s it had become apparent that large sections of American society were being organized around customer satisfaction. Examples include college and university residence

halls, hospitals, retail stores, political campaigns, commercial airlines, and very large Protestant congregations.

In 1970, for example, one congregation constructed a new sanctuary designed to seat 1,000 at worship. The goal was an average attendance of 600 at the first worship service on Sunday morning and an average of 800 at the second. The off-street parking, however, was limited to accommodate 350 cars.

In 1996, another congregation constructed new facilities with three venues for worship. One was a traditional sanctuary designed to seat 500. The second was a big empty box with movable furniture that would accommodate as many as 400 at worship but could be arranged to convey the feeling of "comfortably full" with 150 worshipers. The third room resembled a theater and would seat 300. The weekend worship schedule calls for three Saturday evening worship services, one before the evening meal and two after the meal. The Sunday morning worship calls for seven services beginning with one at 8 o'clock and the last beginning at 11 o'clock. That big box which also serves as a fellowship hall during the rest of the week, houses the 8:00, 9:30, and 11 o'clock services. The other two rooms house the other four. The combined attendance for those ten weekend services averages nearly 2,300. That requires eight acres of off-street parking spaces and interior streets since many of the people also are engaged in seventy-five-minute adult learning communities while others help to staff the Sunday school for children and youth.

That building constructed in 1970 was designed in a producer-driven culture. The newer one was designed in a consumer-driven era. The institutional inability to adapt to that shift in the American population has been one reason some of those very large congregations of the 1960s and 1970s have experienced a decrease in numbers.

6. A relatively rare, but sometimes exceptionally powerful factor has been a change in land use patterns. The construction of a new freeway or the redevelopment of a section of

the city or the replacement of residences with commercial or industrial uses has eliminated what once had been a large part of the natural constituency for an urban church.

7. For many of those former very large Protestant congregations of 1965 or earlier, the most influential factor has been an unwillingness or an inability to compete for future constituents with that growing array of megachurches serving a regional constituency that have been founded since 1970 or with older congregations that chose to relocate to a larger site at a better location in order to begin a new chapter in their history.

If costs and productivity are two of the most influential criteria in designing your turnaround strategy, which should be the higher priority? Providing annual financial subsidies to extend the life expectancy of twenty congregations each averaging fewer than thirty-five at worship? Or enabling one congregation that has been averaging 1,400 at worship to continue to attract newcomers rather than gradually shrink in size?

In other words, one of the most productive components of that larger denominational strategy calls for helping very large congregations to improve their capability to compete for future new constituents. What is the best way to do that? That introduces another high priority.

VII. The Power of Peer Learning

How can a congregation learn how to compete in what is clearly a highly competitive religious environment? The best model was created and perfected by the United States Agricultural Service in the first third of the twentieth century. That also was the model Sam Walton used to create the world's largest chain of retail stores. He never missed an opportunity to study and learn from what his competitors were doing.

How do you persuade a farmer who was living on the edge of economic disaster in the 1930s to purchase new varieties of seed corn, to test the soil and apply the appropriate fertilizer, or to rotate crops? One answer was, "With great difficulty! Farmers prefer to keep on farming the same way their parents farmed."

A better answer was the power of peer learning. A respected farmer was persuaded to adopt the new methods. A few months later the County Agricultural Agent invited nearby farmers to come and spend a couple of hours seeing and hearing "What Ray has done." Most of them left convinced—"If Ray can do it, I can do it."

The power of peer learning has been used for centuries to train recruits in military organizations, to sell clothes to teenage girls, to transform college athletes into professional ball players, to improve the practice of health care, to lower the costs of manufacturing motor vehicles, to train law school graduates, to socialize newcomers into street gangs, and to equip elementary school teachers.

The emergence of self-identified teaching churches in the 1980s represents one of the most hopeful expressions of the power of peer learning in American Protestantism. In the ideal world the leaders of a congregation that finds itself unable to compete with other churches for future new constituents recognizes changes must be made but is uncertain of what to do or how to do it. Those leaders look for and visit a teaching church that "ten years ago resembled who and what we are today, but now is a model of what we believe God is calling our congregation to be and to be doing." They listen to and question both paid and volunteer leaders to discover "how we can learn from what you've done."

Two of the common barriers, however, are polity and community context. Too often that teaching church operates with a different polity and/or is in a sharply different community setting. Those two barriers limit the power of learning from peers.

Despite those two barriers, an affirmation of peer learning and of the role of the self-identified teaching church ranks up there as the seventh most valuable component of a larger strategy if effectiveness and low cost are criteria in designing that turnaround strategy.[6]

VIII. From Geography to Affinity

That affirmation leads to an eighth low-cost component. How does a denominationally affiliated congregation benefit from the power of peer learning when polity and community context can undermine that effort?

The easy answer is to replace geographical proximity with institutional affinity in designing midlevel judicatories. Thus one midlevel judicatory could consist of new congregations founded within the past three or four or five years. Another could consist of those arrangements in which one pastor serves two congregations. A third could be composed of neighborhood churches that have or are in the process of redefining their role. A fourth could be limited to the category we call "Old First Church Downtown." A fifth could be designed for those congregations that are or should be redefining their role from rural to exurban. It would be easy to describe dozens of other affinity midlevel judicatories.

This is *not* a new idea! A hundred years ago the Methodist Episcopal Church consisted of 96 geographically defined annual conferences plus 16 nongeographical affinity and 14 mission conferences. Currently several Protestant denominations that place a high value on being a multicultural religious body are organized with both geographically defined and affinity midlevel judicatories. Examples include the Christian and Missionary Alliance, the Presbyterian Church (USA), and the Southern Baptist Convention.

The real choice, however, for denominational policymakers is not, "Do we want to continue with geographically defined judicatories or do we want to encourage peer learning by the creation of affinity judicatories?" That train left the station more than twenty years ago. The real question today is, "Do we prefer that our congregations benefit from peer learning by relating to churches within our denominational tradition or do we prefer they utilize the resources of teaching churches and parachurch organizations that are outside our denominational tradition?" That train is picking up new passengers every day.

Another advantage offered by this switch to affinity midlevel judicatories is that it can be a useful component in the process of producing better matches between clergy and congregations, for encouraging long pastorates ("What did you do that enabled you to stay in one church for thirty-five years?"), in helping congregations recognize the value of new staff configurations, in offering very large congregations an alternative scenario to numerical decline as well as in designing customized turnaround strategies for midlevel judicatories. It could be argued this adds up to six reasons, including taking advantage of the power of peer learning, why the creation of affinity judicatories should rank first, not eighth, on the changes required to design a turnaround strategy.

IX. Where Will the Babies Born in 1985 Go to Church?

The discussion in this chapter has been organized to describe first what this traveler is convinced meet the two criteria used for ranking the components of a larger strategy. One criterion is the largest return on a modest investment of resources. The second is the degree of difficulty that will be encountered in implementing each facet of that turnaround strategy. Producing better matches between minister and congregation ranks first on both criteria. Adding the option of affinity midlevel judicatories ranks about third on the first criterion, but probably ranks twelfth in most denominations on that second criterion of difficulty.

The next seven components for a turnaround strategy do not promise such a high return on the investment of resources and/or may be far more controversial in ideological terms and/or represent an unacceptable departure from tradition and/or are more difficult to implement and/or may create powerful opposition because "that would invade our turf" and/or generate divisive quarrels over values or what the future will bring.

A large part of the context for discussing these potential components for a turnaround strategy can be summarized by looking at a half dozen "What do you believe?" questions. The answers to these questions will guide the direction of the thinking among the members of your task force as they design a turnaround strategy.

1. What do you believe is the ideal size for a congregation in American Protestantism in the twenty-first century? The simplest answer is an average worship attendance of 100 or fewer. Approximately three out of five congregations fit into that size bracket. If it is the most popular, does that mean it is the ideal? Congregations averaging 100 or fewer at worship outnumber those averaging 350 or more at worship by an 8 to 1 ratio in contemporary American Protestantism. Those averaging 25 or fewer at worship outnumber those averaging 500 or more by more than a 3 to 1 ratio. Does that suggest encouraging more lay-led house churches should be a high priority?

2. A different perspective produces a sharply different question. What do you believe is the minimum size for an American Protestant congregation in the twenty-first century to enable it to both provide an adequate compensation package for a full-time and fully credentialed resident pastor and also challenge that minister in terms of opportunities and work load? Due in part to wide differences in the definition of an "adequate compensation package" (cash salary, housing, utilities, pension, health insurance, continuing education, and professional expenses including automobile allowance), the usual response is an average worship attendance in the 120 to 160 range.

3. Do you believe the ministries that attracted and served the generations born before 1940 will closely resemble the ministries that will be most effective in reaching and serving the generations born in 1985 and later? In other words, will

the turnaround strategy for your denomination focus on extending the past into the future or on designing a new future? In 2005 the median age of the American population age fourteen and over was between forty-one and forty-two years. What is the median age of your membership age 14 and over? In one mainline Protestant denomination that dividing line moved from thirty-eight years in 1965 to fifty-six years in 2005. What do you expect the median will be for the confirmed members (age 14 and over) of your denomination in 2039? If the answer is forty years, that will mean one-half will have been born in 1985 or later.

The American population in 2025 will include at least 80 million people born in those twenty-one years of 1985 through 2005. Some of those 80 million will be immigrants from other parts of this world, but most will have been born in the United States and identify English as their native language.

In 2025 these 80 million residents in that twenty to forty age cohort will have many choices if and when they look for a church home. Let us assume that only one-half will have found the church home they have been seeking by the end of 2025. That will be 40 million "young" adults. How many is 40 million? That number is the equivalent to the combined total average worship attendance of all ages in 2005 for the Roman Catholic Church in America, the Southern Baptist Convention, The United Methodist Church, The Evangelical Lutheran Church in America, the Presbyterian Church (USA), the Lutheran Church-Missouri Synod, the Episcopal Church USA, the American Baptist Churches USA, the United Church of Christ, and the Christian Church (Disciples of Christ).

4. As you design an evangelistic strategy to reach this population born in the 1985–2005 era, what do you believe are among the most important variables?

From this observer's perspective seven stand out. The first is that many of the older members of this generation place a high value on religion. Child Trends, a research organization, reports three out of five teenagers indicate religion is either "very important" or "pretty important" to them. The number of Bible Clubs meeting in high schools keeps setting new records year after year. Researchers at university medical schools such as Dartmouth, UCLA, and Harvard have commented on the impact of religion on the lives of teenagers. High school graduates are enrolling in Christ-centered colleges in record numbers.

Second, the churches that project high expectations of teenagers currently appear to be attracting the largest numbers of youth born in the 1985–1990 era. Competition is more attractive than boredom.

Third, the public schools in general, and the large public high schools in particular, have socialized today's children and youth how to live and function in a very large, complex, and anonymous social system. While some of the outcomes have been less than fully desirable, that is a fact of contemporary reality. There is a vast difference between attending a high school with an enrollment under 250, the dominant pattern of the 1930s, and one with an enrollment in the 1,000 to 5,000 range![7]

Fourth, thanks to television, computers, and video games, visual communication has moved far ahead of oral communication in grabbing and holding the attention of today's teenagers.

Fifth, in building their personal social network or friendship circle, today's teenagers give a low priority to place of residence and place a high value on points of commonality such as skin color, language, hobbies, and other interests. Today's seventeen-year-old is far more likely to travel from Point A to Point B by motor vehicle than by walking or a bicycle. That geographically large public school district is more influential than a geographically defined neighborhood or kinship ties in defining the candidates for a teenager's personal social network.

Sixth, consumerism is a distinctive force in the contemporary American economy and teenagers are not an exception. One consequence is "a meaningful response to my needs" often ranks above inherited denominational loyalties in choosing a church home.

Seventh, for many teenagers, peer pressure outranks either parental advice or inherited institutional loyalties in making decisions. This probably will raise the level of competition among the Christian congregations in the United States to attract and retain the allegiance of that age cohort born in the 1985–2005 era. Will the turnaround strategy for your denomination place a high priority on ministries with these younger adults of 2025?

5. What do you believe the church shoppers of 2025 will be seeking as they look for a new church home? The most reliable response, of course, is, "Ask me that question in 2027 after it has been researched." A better answer, however, is, "We can't plan for the future unless we first agree on our assumptions about what the future will bring." One example of that is, "Do we assume the geographical proximity of the place of residence to the place of worship will be less influential in 2025 than it was in 1925 or 1955?"

A third response is to look at the explanations given by three American-born white males who were regular church attendees in 2005. The oldest of the three, Fred Baxter, was born in 1936 and told this story.

"I retired in 2001. My wife and I have been members of the same congregation for the past thirty years. Nearly every Sunday found us in the same adult Sunday school class. After that, we went to church. After the kids left home, on most Sundays we went out to lunch with friends from that class. One Sunday at lunch, one of our friends in that class, Jack Adams, told us that he had signed up to go as a short-term volunteer missionary to our sister church in Peru. As we drove home, my wife told me, 'Fred, you ought to sign up for that mission trip. It would be good for you!' I protested I was too old. She said that if Jack Adams, who was three years older than I, could go, I could go. After a couple of weeks, I finally decided to sign up for that trip. There were eleven members from our church who made the trip. We were gone for thirteen days. We spent eleven days working with fellow Christians in that sister church. That experience transformed my life! While I was there, I realized that while I called myself a Christian, I really was a nominal believer. I left home a believer and came back a committed disciple of Jesus Christ. I've been back to Peru twice, and I can't wait until spring when we return for our next visit. Some of my closest friends today are members of that sister church of ours in Peru."

When Mrs. Baxter was asked about Fred's experiences in Peru, she replied, "Each year I get back a different husband than the man I sent, but it's always an improvement!"

Michael Zimmerman was born in 1966. He told a different story. "Fifteen years ago I married my wife who had been reared as a fourth-generation Roman Catholic. I had been raised Baptist, so we decided that after we were married, we would look for a church home that would be new to both of us. On the recommendation of a friend, we visited a Methodist Church one Sunday morning. We both liked the minister and after another couple of months of church shopping, we returned there and eventually joined it. We went to church nearly every Sunday morning, but that was the extent of our involvement. My wife took most of the responsibility for raising our kids. I had a good job, but it required a lot of travel. In the fall of 2004, the church announced the formation of several new study groups. Each group was committed to spend forty days studying Rick Warren's book *The Purpose-Driven Life* and to meet together weekly. We met and made some new friends as well as became much closer to those friends who had persuaded us to join it. While I'm not a Calvinist, those forty days of study transformed our lives and also strengthened our marriage. By the time we finished that class, my wife and I both realized we had been drifting through life on a week-to-week and month-to-month basis. That class gave us the structure we needed to be more intentional about our relationships with God, with one another as a husband-wife couple, about our roles as parents, and, most important, as committed Christians. We were regular churchgoers when we signed up for that class. Today we're well on the road to becoming deeply devoted followers of Jesus Christ."

Matthew West was born in 1988. By the fall of 2004 it was clear to Matthew's parents that he was a bored high school junior who was looking forward to completion of what he described as "my four-year sentence to prison for the crime of turning fourteen back in 2002." The four-year high school Matthew attended has an enrollment of slightly over 2,800 teenagers. Approximately 900 students are actively engaged in one or more structured extracurricular activities such as highly competitive interscholastic sports including football and basketball, the school newspaper, the marching band, drama, forensics, clubs, school governance, the high school annual, and track and field. An overlapping 1,200 find considerable personal satisfactions, as well as financial income, from their part-time jobs on weekends or after school. One seventeen-year-old described his life as "I work two jobs, school and at the supermarket. My paycheck gives me better and more frequent feedback on how I'm doing than does my report card."

Matthew also lives in two worlds. One is five days every week at school. Matthew does not participate in any extracurricular activities, nor does he hold a job during the school year. He has been a straight A student ever since fifth grade. He spends about thirty to forty hours a week in the virtual world of computer and video games. Matthew owns an Xbox™ console. This magic box has enabled Matthew to graduate from the simple switch speed reflex games of the video arcade to highly complex games that require up to fifty hours of concentrated thought and effort to finish. He also likes online multiplayer games that last as long as he is able to be engaged by new challenges and may continue in that ever evolving game for several months.[8]

When asked how his parents view his hobby, Matthew explained, "They don't care how much time I spend playing video games as long as I keep my grades up. And that's not hard, not with the classes at my high school. That's why I like the video games that challenge me to figure out how to beat it, but I always do. Then I move on to the next level, which is even harder, but it's satisfying to know that I'm mastering the game. Sometimes I really get into a game and will design a new level for other people to play, and it's like I'm a game designer, too. If it's a really good level, I may even include it in the next version of the game. Occasionally I'll get a game that I can finish in a weekend easy. That's really lame, almost as lame as my classes. I like games that make me think and really work at them. Otherwise, why bother?"

What do those three reflections from three different white American-born males from three different generations have in common? First, all three illustrate the point that we are now living in a culture that places a high value on meaningful and memorable experiences.[9] Two describe real-world experiences while Matthew's experiences are in the virtual world. Second, those are transformational experiences. Fred Baxter's life was transformed by his short-term missionary experiences in another culture. Michael Zimmerman's faith journey was transformed by a challenging study program that he shared with his wife and several peers. Matthew West experienced intellectual growth by new challenges in the virtual world.

Third, all three have experienced the excitement of learning that has moved them to a new level of life. One consequence is a lowered tolerance for boring experiences. Fourth, all three conceptualize life as a journey enriched by anticipation of a new tomorrow.

Fifth, not one of these three is likely to be attracted to a church in which next Sunday morning's worship service is likely, with modest changes, to be a carbon copy of last Sunday's service that closely resembled the previous Sunday's service. All three are more likely to be interested in worship that is designed to be a meaningful and memorable experience rather than a "service," that challenges passive believers to become active disciples, and that introduces alternative ways to equip worshipers for ministry.

One response to this scenario could be, "That is simply the definition of a good church. Therefore one of our goals should be to increase the number of good churches in our denomination."

The best response to that comment is found in the first line of the first chapter of a recent best-selling book by Jim Collins, "Good is the enemy of great."[10]

Which churches in 2025 will attract the largest proportion of the churchgoers born in 2005 and earlier?

Those congregations that possess the sophisticated software required to communicate the heart of the Christian faith, as well as the story of the Christian church, to young people like Matthew West on their level of learning will have a great advantage over those that rely on oral communication or on the printed word. Where is that seventeen-year-old in your denomination who will create that software for your churches by 2009?

This observer is convinced the answer will be those congregations that are able to reach, attract, serve, nurture, assimilate, and challenge the counterparts of Fred Baxter, Michael Zimmerman, and Matthew West. That will require a combination of visionary leadership and sensitivity to the fact that people are not all at the same stage of their personal faith journey plus the resources required to offer people a variety of meaningful and memorable experiences.

That is a big assignment! Relatively few congregations that average fewer than 500 at weekend worship will be able to mobilize all those resources. That introduces the last of these six questions.

6. Do you believe large institutions, such as supermarkets, hospitals, universities, farms, financial institutions, bookstores, discount stores, medical clinics, and Protestant megachurches will continue to dominate the American economy in the twenty-first century?

This observer's guess is future generations of American churchgoers will bring both a larger quantity and a greater variety of expectations to church than currently are being brought by today's adults. Therefore the demand will be for congregations that are able to mobilize the resources required to meet those expectations. Today that usually means an average worship attendance for the weekend of at least 500. Therefore a high-priority component of that larger denominational strategy could be to encourage the emergence of more large and very large congregations.

An attainable goal has been reached by one of the oldest denominations in American Christianity—the Reformed Church in America—and by one of the newest—the Assemblies of God—as well as by the Baptist General Conference, the Evangelical Covenant Church, the Evangelical Free Church in America, the Lutheran Church-Missouri Synod, and the Wisconsin Evangelical Lutheran Synod. That goal is 4 percent of all congregations average 500 or more at worship.

A modest compatible goal would be at least 2 percent average 800 or more at worship.

One way to do that is to plant new missions designed to average at least 500 at worship within a year or two following that first public worship service. Another tactic includes better matches and longer pastorates. A crucial factor is the appropriate staff configuration. Another could be the creation of an affinity judicatory open to (a) congregations averaging 350 to 800 at worship who have both the potential and the desire to double in size and (b) a dozen or more very large congregations that have doubled their average worship attendance during the past decade and are able and willing to accept a role as teaching churches. One high potential possibility is to encourage numerically growing congregations that are considering enlarging their present site or relocating to a ten to twenty-acre parcel of land to consider purchasing a 40 to 400-acre site for relocation and become a destination church.

A huge potential fringe benefit could be that one out of seven of those very large churches could and would accept the role as a teaching church. These teaching churches would resource part of that emphasis on peer learning described earlier. In addition, they could provide a valuable postseminary apprenticeship of ten to twelve years for persons who display the passion, gifts, and personality, and who promise to become the team leader for a megachurch.

The big barrier, however, may be the objections of those who are ideologically opposed to large congregations and/or see the megachurch as a threat to the future of the small and midsized congregations. In terms of return on the investment of denominational resources, it could be argued that encouraging the emergence of more very large congregations should be the top priority in a denominational strategy. One reason it is ranked so low rather than first is the shortage of pastors with the gifts, personality, skills, vision, passion, experience, and leadership required to make it happen. A second is the shortage of people for the necessary staff configuration. A third is an ideological opposition to a megachurch. A fourth is a shortage of good sites. A fifth is the plea, "Instead of allocating scarce denominational resources to help those big, strong, and fortunate churches that don't need help, why don't we direct those resources to helping our small, struggling congregations?"

X. The Multisite Option

In the middle of this list is the component for that denominational turnover strategy that requires the smallest investment of denominational resources and is relatively easy to

119

implement. It is placed tenth, rather than first in this chapter, because it represents the greatest conflict with tradition and also requires an exceptionally high level of entrepreneurial enthusiasm. That explains why (a) currently it is a more popular option with independent churches and in denominations with a congregational polity than with congregations in which the denomination exercises a powerful regulatory role and (b) it requires a separate chapter. (See chapter 4.)

XI. Relocation

The most common ceiling that limits the evangelistic outreach and the potential numerical growth among congregations in contemporary American Protestantism is the reluctance of the current members to make the changes required to reach new generations of people. Second is the barrier created by short pastorates, many of which are a consequence of mismatches between minister and congregation. Instead of increasing their competence in evangelism, many of these congregations concentrate on enhancing their skills in planning farewell events for the departing pastor and/or designing a reception for the successor. Third is the national shortage of ministers who excel as transformational leaders. Fourth is the power of intradenominational quarreling to attract more players than that game called evangelism.

About fifth on this list is the simple fact that more than one-half of all congregations in American Protestantism are limited by their real estate. They gather in what today is a functionally obsolete building and/or at what is an inadequate site and/or at what today is not a desirable location in terms of accessibility, visibility, and the adjacent land uses. Many complain, "We're only three hundred feet from what would be an excellent location." Others worship in a second-floor room designed by men who expected to die before they became too old to climb stairs. Tens of thousands gather in a room designed for a presentation approach to worship that is not suitable for participatory worship. Many more are limited by a shortage of off-street parking or the absence of a gymnasium or a shortage of multiple purpose meeting rooms.

A common, but excessively simplistic diagnosis is, "This congregation has two choices. It can go down the road to oblivion by continuing to meet in this building on this site at this location or it can plan for a new tomorrow in new facilities on a larger site at a better location."

Eventually a detailed proposal is presented to the members and a congregational meeting is called to vote on the issue. The result is that relocation is defeated by a vote of 60 percent opposed and only 40 percent supporting it.

Why did that happen? The most frequent explanation is the issue appeared to focus on real estate, but it really was about change. In the absence of a widely perceived crisis, the normal, natural, and predictable response to a new idea is to reject it. That is the safe decision! If it really is a good idea, it will be presented again and again. If it is not a good idea, it should be rejected.

Therefore the appropriate response to that initial rejection should consist of three questions. First, did we present it prematurely? Frequently the proponents of change assume that what appears to them to be the only prudent course of action will automatically earn the required support on its merits. In real life the followers may need more time to talk themselves into supporting change than was required by those generating that proposal. The task force that created the relocation plan may have required eighteen months to agree on it, but only four months are scheduled between the submission of their recommendation and the date of that congregational vote. That raises the second question, if this vote was either premature or was the natural response to a new idea when it is first presented, when do we bring it up for a second vote?

Third, did we state the question properly? Frequently the question presented for a congregational vote is stated as, "Do you favor or oppose relocation?" Since the natural response to any proposal for change is to oppose it, that loads the question in favor of disapproval. The physician's diagnosis calls for surgery. One way to present that to the patient is the statement, "I believe you need surgery." A better statement could be, "Our diagnosis indicates you have two choices. One is surgery. The other is you probably will die within four to six months."

Instead of asking for a yes or no vote on a proposal for relocation, a fairer statement could be, "Do you prefer a continued aging and numerical shrinkage of our membership by continuing to meet in these facilities at this location or do you favor creating a new tomorrow for our congregation in new physical facilities at a larger site and a better location?"

If the leaders are absolutely convinced relocation is the only viable option, the question at that congregational meeting could be, "Do you favor relocating our meeting place to Site A or to Site B?" One way leaders lead is by how they state the question.

A review of the outcomes of scores of congregations that have completed a productive relocation plan is that the first step in the process consists of recognizing the need to relocate. A common second step is the appointment of a task force to design a relocation plan. A common third step is the rejection of relocation at a congregational meeting. The fourth step is to define that rejection as a necessary component of the larger process and to bring in a new action plan. If God gives sinful human beings a second chance, is it too much to expect that congregational leaders will give the members a second chance?

Early in the process of planning for the relocation of the meeting place, three other questions should be addressed. First, is relocation motivated primarily by a desire to attempt to "follow our members as they move to newer and better housing"? This was a driving motivation in the second half of the twentieth century as Jewish congregations relocated to follow their members, as black congregations relocated to follow their upwardly mobile members, as Swedish Baptist, Norwegian Lutheran, and upper middle class Methodist, United Church of Christ, Presbyterian, and other congregations relocated to follow their members. Or is the primary motivation a desire to perpetuate yesterday with new generations of "our kind of people" at a new location? Or is the primary motivation to create a new tomorrow at a new location with a new constituency?

One implication is the projected size of the future congregation. If this congregation enjoyed a peak average worship attendance of 450 and now averages 210, does the relocation plan call for a congregation that will average 500 at worship? Or 210? Or 700? Or 1,200? A common pattern is to design a building for a congregation averaging 1,200 at worship, but include financing for a staff sufficient to serve a congregation averaging 350 at worship. The result is an understaffed, largely empty, and heavily mortgaged building.

A second implication concerns the name. The Euclid Avenue Church, the Church Street Church, and the Park Avenue Church are examples of three congregations that relocated to a new street but carried the old name to that new address. One reason *not* to change the name is to avoid overloading the system with too many changes at one time. If, however, the motivation for relocation is to create a new congregation with new physical facilities at a new location to reach and serve a new constituency, a change of name may be appropriate. Which is the stronger influence? To maintain continuity with the past? Or to affirm discontinuity?

A more sensitive issue is the staff configuration. Once again continuity is a factor. The basic generalization is the larger the size of the congregation and/or the shorter the period of time it has been meeting at the current address and/or the faster the recent influx of new people and/or the longer the tenure of the current pastor, the greater the proportion of the institutional continuity is in the current minister or senior pastor. By contrast, in the congregation that has been meeting at this same address since before 1940, has been experiencing an aging and shrinking of the membership, displays a strong denominational affiliation, and worships in a room filled with decades of sacred memories, only a relatively small proportion of the continuity is in the person of that minister whom they welcomed a couple of years ago.

Therefore, if the driving force behind the decision is to perpetuate the past, it may be appropriate to retain the services of that long tenured senior minister. Likewise, if the pastor, regardless of tenure, was the number one advocate of relocation, it may be wise to seek to retain the services of that minister for at least several years after the move to the new address. On the other hand, if the driving motivation is to create a new tomorrow at a new location with a new constituency, it may be appropriate to design a new staff configuration for that new ministry plan. That new staff configuration may or may not include the current pastor. A more common consequence of relocation is at the new site that relocated congregation outgrows the capability of one or more staff members to adapt to that new era.

Finally, what are the implications for those policy-making positions filled by lay volunteers? A useful guideline is the greater the desire to reach and serve a younger constituency and/or to reverse years of numerical decline and/or to fill a new role in ministry and/or to house a new ministry plan, the more important it is that these volunteer policy-makers display at least six of these nine characteristics: first, they were committed advocates of relocation. Second, they bring a powerful future orientation to that policy-making role. Third, they were born after 1960. Fourth, they are relatively recent new members of this congregation. Fifth, they have earned the respect of long tenured volunteers. Sixth, they place a high value on evangelism. Seventh, they are persuasive leaders. Eighth, they are unreserved supporters of the current pastor. Ninth, they recognize that famous sentence, "If we build it, they will come" may be an attractive theme for a motion picture or for a tourist stop, but those words also can be found on a prominent signpost on the road to disappointment in a congregation's relocation effort.

In summary, the experiences of congregations that have relocated their meeting place since 1980 have provided us with two sets of lessons. One set describes how this can be an alternative filled with disappointments. The other set describes how relocation can be a highly productive component of a larger denominational turnaround strategy. Therefore that nongeographical affinity judicatory designed for congregations contemplating relocation of their meeting place should include two or three congregations that have had less than a completely satisfying experience with relocation. It also should include seven or eight successful experiences by congregations that will accept that role as teaching churches. We can learn from both success and failure. One lesson common to both groups is expressed in this reflection, "If we had it to do over again, we would have purchased a larger relocation site." A second frequently stated lesson, "Our first master plan for construction included only one option for a second building program and only one option for a third building program. If we had it to do over again, we would insist that the master plan include at least four alternatives for the second construction phase." A common third lesson is, "We seriously underestimated how much parking we would need, and that has caused first-time visitors to drive in and immediately depart when they could not find a vacant parking space."

One reason for placing relocation as the eleventh component in this discussion is that while it often can be a highly productive return on a modest investment of denominational resources, it also is a far more complicated undertaking today than it was four or five decades ago.

XII. Plant New Missions!

In the last two decades of the nineteenth century, 1880–1899, the two dozen Lutheran denominations in the

United States planted a combined total of 4,932 new congregations that were still in existence in 1906 when the United States Bureau of the Census conducted that comprehensive census of religious bodies. That averages out to 246 per year for twenty years. A reasonable guess is the actual number was closer to 270 per year since an unknown number of those new missions did not survive until 1906. The four predecessors of today's United Church of Christ launched an average of at least 150 new churches annually during those two decades. The Protestant Episcopal Church started an average of more than 100 missions every year; the twelve Presbyterian denominations organized a combined annual average of 235 new churches, the six predecessor denominations of what today is The United Methodist Church started a combined average of 720 new congregations annually; the Christian Church (Disciples of Christ) launched an average of 136 annually; the Northern Baptists averaged 125 a year while the Southern Baptists averaged 350 annually; the Seventh-day Adventists averaged 40 per year; the African Methodist Episcopal Church averaged 120 annually; the Colored Methodist Episcopal Church averaged 40 new churches annually; the AME Zion averaged close to 40; the Reformed Church in America averaged 19; the Christian Reformed Church averaged 8; the Salvation Army averaged 20; the Universalists averaged 9; and the Unitarians averaged about 7 new congregations annually.

In order to be counted, all of those new churches had to be in existence for at least seven years, so those numbers clearly understate the trend. It also should be noted that during the 1880 to 1899 period, the population of the United States increased by an average of 1.2 million annually. That compares with an average yearly increase of 3 million during the 1995–2005 era. The number of adult residents of the United States not actively involved in the life of any religious community in 2000 exceeded the total population of this country in 1880.

The ratio of Protestant churches to population in the United States in 1890 was one congregation for approximately every 400 residents. Today that ratio is one Protestant congregation for every 900 residents.

Add to that array of historical statistics the fact that several of the mainline Protestant denominations in the United States have reduced the number of affiliated congregations by 10 to 50 percent since 1906 and it is easy to see why many professionals in the Church Growth Movement contend that planting more new missions should be the number one component of a denominational turnaround strategy.

Why is it placed near the middle in this chapter? First, the failure rate today is fairly high. This observer's sample of that universe suggests that fewer than one-half of all new denominationally affiliated Protestant congregations launched during the 1985–1994 decade achieved these three criteria for success: (a) they were still in existence ten years after that first public worship service, (b) they were averaging at least 125 at worship by the end of year five of their existence, and (c) they became financially self-supporting within three years. It is far more difficult to launch what will become a self-governing, self-financing, self-expressing, and self-propagating new mission today than it was in the 1880s or 1950s.

Second, the resources required to be competitive in terms of money, real estate, staff, and program are far greater than was the case as recently as the 1960s. In other words, this component of a denominational strategy ranks relatively low if costs and the chances of success are the criteria used to evaluate it. Third, today we see dozens of different models being used. That is the big reason why this option deserves a separate chapter. (See chapter 5.)

XIII. Trust and Empower the Laity!

When the adult population of the United States of 2000 is compared with the adult population of 1900, four differences stand out for this discussion. First, a far larger proportion has completed at least eight years of formal education beyond the eighth grade. As recently as 1940 it was not unusual for the pastor with both college and seminary degrees to be not only the best educated person in that congregation but also one of only two or three persons in the entire community with two academic degrees. Today it is not unusual for the pastor with two academic degrees to be serving a congregation in which scores of adults have completed more years of formal education. More important, many of the laity have both more training and greater skill in managing an organization designed to provide person-centered services than does that pastor. Second, the number of deeply committed Christian laypersons with two or three decades of successful experience as venturesome and creative entrepreneurs has increased at least twenty times since 1900.

Third, the number of years between retirement from the secular labor force and death, or between retirement and a life limited by severe physical disabilities, has increased greatly. The current population of the United States includes millions of adults in the 55 to 75 age bracket who have retired from the active labor force, who continue to receive a comfortable annual income, who enjoy excellent physical and mental health, and who are ready for a new challenge. Many of these are deeply committed Christians who feel a call from God to Christian ministry. The majority, of course, are women, but at least one-third are men. A tiny fraction decide to enroll in a theological seminary, but the vast majority do not see that as the next stage in their life journey. Many have decades of experience as self-taught lifelong learners.

Fourth, for the first half of the twentieth century the most common synonym for "poor" was "elderly." Today that synonym is "child." Currently the second wealthiest age cohort in the United States consists of Americans age 65 to 69. The only wealthier age group are Americans age 70 to 74.

This population, especially in those denominations that have focused on mature adults as their core constituency in recent years, constitutes a huge and underutilized resource.

One consequence is the increased reliance on requests for proposals for new church development as described in chapter 5. More significant is the creation of lay teams to staff off-campus ministries as described in chapter 4. While not the most significant, one of the most impressive is when a half dozen laypersons come together to create a plan for a new ministry that will cost a million dollars or more to implement. Within a few months they have raised the necessary funds. The rapid growth in the number of lay-led house churches in upper middle class suburbia is another example. The creation of a team of three to five lay professionals to conduct the annual performance audit of that regional judicatory is another, although to some of the clergy, that belongs in the category of the most threatening consequences. Perhaps the most common is the megachurch with a paid program staff consisting of two full-time ordained ministers, two part-time program staff positions filled by two semiretired ordained ministers, two full-time lay program generalists, plus five full-time lay specialists and a dozen part-time, most of whom are semiretired from the secular labor force, lay specialists. A large proportion of the total workload is carried by scores of mature lay volunteers.

The reason this is not placed among the top four or five components of a turnaround strategy is a clergy-dominated denominational culture makes it difficult to both trust and challenge the laity. That helps to explain why most of the outstanding models of the empowerment of the laity can be found in the nondenominational megachurches.

XIV. Encourage Lay-led House Churches

Back in the early years following the end of World War II, most lay-led house churches fell into one of three categories. One consisted of low-income American-born residents with a Western European ancestry who (a) perceived they would not be welcomed if they attempted to enter those intimidating buildings housing established white middle class Protestant congregations and (b) since they had little or no control over most aspects of life, wanted to control how and where they gathered for the corporate worship of God. A second group of house churches were the creation of American-born black Christians. A third consisted of recent immigrants who wanted to worship God in their native language and their native culture and could not afford to own and maintain a separate building reserved for religious uses 365 days a year.

In recent years an uncounted number of new house churches have been created by middle and upper class white Americans who prefer the intimacy, the absence of complexity, the unreserved complete local control, and the informality of the house church. Most of these families live in a residence that includes an attractive room that can accommodate seven to fifteen worshipers comfortably. More than a few, when interviewed, express values and feelings that could be described as anticlericalism and/or antidenominationalism. They often add they are able to fulfill their goals that between 75 and 100 percent of their financial contributions, which often are very generous, should go directly to worthy Christian missional causes and/or worthy Christian organizations. Most also feel very strongly that they have something between an obligation and a right to decide on the recipients of those charitable dollars. They do not express a need to delegate that responsibility to a third party!

How do house churches fit into a denominationally designed turnaround strategy? One option is to encourage interested laypersons to create new ones with a built-in relationship to that denomination.

A second is to offer to adopt existing house churches as legitimate expressions of God's creation. Invite them to become a part of your denominational system. That usually will require a few innovative adjustments, but it can be done. One reason it should be considered is that several of today's nondenominational megachurches trace their origins back to the day when they began as lay-led house churches. If you believe that one reason for the existence of denominational systems is to facilitate the concept of the interdependence of Christian congregations, that is the primary justification for this invitation. (That position can be documented in the writings of Saint Paul.)

A third option is to encourage larger congregations with discretionary resources to create new house churches as a part of their evangelistic outreach. The best-documented expression is the Key Church Strategy that originated in the Southern Baptist Convention in 1979. While it was not conceptualized as house churches, the implementation for the Key Church Strategy often created what in essence became lay-led house churches.[11] The Key Church Strategy stands out as an exceptionally effective way for congregations and/or denominational agencies owned and operated by and for adults from the upper half of the social class ladder to reach and serve people living on the lowest rungs of that ladder.

In broader terms house churches represent an effective way for the institutional expressions of the Christian church, such as denominations and congregations, to reach and be heard by anti-institutionalists with the good news that Jesus is Lord and Savior.

If it is so effective, why is it placed so far from the beginning in this chapter? One reason is it carries the double stigma of "Not invented here" and "We've never done it that way." A second reason was discussed earlier. Implementation required unreserved trust in the commitment, the creativity, and the competence of the laity. A third reason is many denominational leaders do not perceive house churches to be in that toolbox labeled "Missions and Evangelism." Instead, house churches often are perceived to be rivals, competitors, aliens, or even possibly the enemy.

XV. Integrate Our Anglo Congregations

Back in the 1960s a substantial number of white Protestant church leaders became deeply committed to the racial integration of white congregations.[12] By 1965 it had become apparent there were at least two incompatible positions on this subject. One was advocated by white Protestants who insisted that every congregation should welcome Negroes (to use the most widely used polite descriptive term of that day) as full and equal members. A different perspective was offered by the pastors of Negro congregations. One described it to me in these words, "What you are advocating is creaming off most of our younger and upwardly mobile members, many of whom are among our best leaders, in order to alleviate your feelings of guilt over racial segregation in America. The inevitable result is this will destroy the strongest institution in the black community."

At that time it was widely assumed that the burden for the racial integration of the predominantly white institutions in America, such as service clubs, lodges, professional associations, churches, public schools, colleges and universities, restaurants, radio stations, professional sports teams, newspapers, and the corporate boardroom rested on the people who traced their ancestry back to Africa. They should be the pioneers who joined previously all-white groups. Only rarely was it suggested, even in the twenty-first century, that whites should join black institutions.[13]

Long before the end of the twentieth century it had become apparent that the support for the ethnic integration of predominantly white institutions in America had been eroded by a growing demand for ethnic self-determination and ethnic separation. This was *not* a new pattern! On the religious scene in the eighteenth and nineteenth centuries Lutherans, Roman Catholics, Methodists, Baptists, and adherents of other religions who immigrated from Europe to the United States created their own congregations to serve a single immigrant group. Lutherans, Baptists, the Reformed, and the Evangelicals took the process to another level and organized Norwegian or German or Swedish or Dutch or Finnish denominations in America. The Methodist Episcopal Church was one of several denominations to welcome immigrants by organizing nongeographical affinity midlevel judicatories. Among the questions raised by this potential component of a denominational strategy are these five.

1. Is the goal to reach and attract integrationists or separatists? Most recent immigrants and a majority of American-born black churchgoers tend to be separatists.[14]
2. Is the goal to integrate predominantly white congregations that are affiliated with an overwhelmingly white regional judicatory? Or does that goal include creating nongeographical midlevel judicatories consisting only of racially and/or culturally integrated congregations? In other words, what is the institutional support system for integrating the predominantly white congregations?
3. If the goal is to create congregations that include English-speaking Anglo members as well as recent immigrants from Latin America, Africa, and the Pacific Rim, does this mean the pastor and other program staff members must be fluent in Korean, Spanish, Twi, Mandarin, and three or four other languages as well as in English?
4. Does the demand for members of racial and ethnic minority groups in the United States to come and join predominantly white congregations exceed the supply of integrationists who are convinced the time has come for American Protestantism to be a color-free religion?
5. Perhaps most important of all, what has been the most effective way to motivate members of racial and ethnic minorities to venture forth and join all-white or predominantly white congregations?

At the top of what is a fairly long list of positive experiences has been the Christian day school operated by a white congregation that has been able to attract American-born black students. If that school is designed to be the central component of a larger package of ministries offered to parents under the slogan, "We're here to help you rear your children in a Christian community," that can be an effective way to racially integrate what had been an all-Anglo congregation. If the school is designed as a community service project, that can be a significant contribution, but only a minor factor in integrating that parish.

If the goal is to attract couples in a bicultural marriage, a powerful and attractive symbol is the pastor who is married to a spouse from a different racial or nationality heritage. The Anglo pastor with a Chinese wife is one example.

In other words, posting a sign on the front door of the church declaring, "We welcome everyone" usually is not the crucial action leading to integration. The all-white congregation worshiping in a building located in a neighborhood that today is occupied by recent immigrants from Latin America or from the Pacific Rim that calls an American black pastor is placing a huge load on that minister's shoulders! That tactic is far more likely to be a success story if five or ten years earlier that congregation had welcomed black children into its Christian day school.

If the goal of that predominantly Anglo congregation is to attract immigrants from Guatemala, a productive tactic is to build a sister church relationship with one or more Protestant congregations in Guatemala with teams of lay volunteers spending ten to fifteen days as short-term missionaries with their fellow Christians in those sister churches every year. The power of common experiences cannot be overstated! "You mean you've been to the community where I was born?" can open doors across cultural barriers.

This possible component of a turnaround strategy can bring rich rewards, but it is difficult to implement. The merger agreement of 1987 that created the Evangelical Lutheran Church in America included a goal that by 1997 at least 10 percent of the members of this new denomination would be persons of color or individuals whose first language was not English. It is possible that goal will be achieved by 2007, but more time may be required.

If the goal is to attract as future new members persons from an ethnic minority group or recent immigrants, the predominantly Anglo American Protestant denominations with the best success stories tend to (a) be located near the legal principles end of that spectrum described in chapter 2 and/or (b) encourage congregations to operate Christian day schools and/or (c) have a long record of organizing new congregations in those countries from which recent immigrants to the United States were born and/or (d) include monocultural midlevel judicatories and/or (e) adhere to an unambiguous and clearly stated doctrinal position and/or (f) place a high value on indigenous leadership including welcoming pastors who served that same general constituency in another part of the world before coming to America.

XVI. Staffing Small Congregations

One-half of the congregations in American Protestantism average fewer than 80 at worship and approximately two-thirds average 125 or fewer. Given the recent increases in the total compensation (cash salary, housing, utilities, pension, health insurance, continuing education, et al.), most congregations averaging fewer than 125 at worship cannot afford the financial costs of being able to attract and retain the services of a full-time and fully credentialed pastor. If the goal is to help small churches fulfill their potential and double, triple, or quadruple their numbers, that usually requires a pastorate of at least ten to fifteen years. That eliminates the options of (a) the typical one- to four-year postseminary apprenticeship and (b) the three- to five-year preretirement pastorate.

One option is the married couple in which the lay spouse has a permanent job in that community and earns employer-paid health insurance covering the whole family. The ordained spouse becomes available to serve as the pastor of that small congregation. That is but one of a growing number of alternatives for providing ministerial leadership for small-membership churches.[15] That, however, is not the issue to be discussed here. The question here is, what are the expectations in that denominational turnaround strategy for these small congregations? Most of those expectations fit into one of a half dozen categories.

1. The goal is to provide a maintenance type of staffing. Hopefully this approach will enable these congregations to more or less remain on a plateau in size while providing an adequate level of ministerial services at a cost that congregation can afford.

The recent rapid increase in the number of middle-aged adults who are eager to serve as licensed lay pastors is one attractive alternative. Frequently the result can be an eight- to fifteen-year pastorate. Since high-quality, meaningful, and continuing interpersonal relationships constitute much of the glue that holds the people together in these small churches, this usually turns out to be a better arrangement than a series of two- or three-year part-time student pastorates.

2. Over the typical five year period a majority of American Protestant congregations averaging fewer than 50 at worship report a decrease in their average attendance. Therefore the long-term goal for these small churches in that denominational strategy is their eventual dissolution and the sale of the real estate. The historical record suggests that two of the most heavily traveled roads to dissolution are (a) a series of brief part-time pastorates by a passing parade of student ministers, and (b) relying on one minister to serve concurrently as the pastor of two or three or four or five small congregations.

3. The operational strategy for that denomination calls for a gradual withdrawal from that metropolitan area or that county or that state. Seven of the most effective ways to

implement that strategy are relevant to this discussion. The first is to create a series of mismatches between pastor and congregations that encourage internal conflict, short pastorates, and bitter terminations. Second, encourage a series of short-term pastorates by part-time student ministers. Third, in order to affirm a denominational emphasis on theological pluralism, encourage short pastorates in which the theologically liberal minister is followed by an evangelical who, a few years later, is followed by a unitarian who is succeeded by another evangelical who is followed by a universalist, etc. Fourth, if new missions are launched, use a design that produces a congregation that plateaus with an average worship attendance of fewer than one hundred. Fifth, encourage smaller congregations to share a pastor with one or two or three other congregations, preferably with at least two different denominations in that cooperative arrangement. That helps to blur the denominational identity and makes it easier for members to switch their allegiance to a new nondenominational congregation. Sixth, subsidize those small congregations, either directly or indirectly, through paying part of the pastor's compensation, such as health insurance or pension payments, through the denominational budget. This builds a dependency relationship. After three or four years, terminate the subsidy and encourage that congregation to choose between merger and dissolution. The seventh is the most highly visible. Encourage two small congregations to merge. In the vast majority of congregational mergers, as in most denominational mergers, 8 plus 4 usually produces a result somewhere between 4 and 10. From a long-term perspective this can turn out to be one of the three or four most effective ways to implement that withdrawal strategy. (The two most effective are a complete and permanent moratorium on planting new missions and generating mismatches in ministerial placement.)

4. A central goal of that denominational turnaround strategy is to include all ages in the total constituency. One way

to achieve that goal is to expand the range of choices available to people. High on that list of options is the possibility of being a member of a small to midsized worshiping community that encourages intimacy and minimizes complexity and also have access to all the ministries and programs that require the resources that can be mobilized only by huge congregations. The members of the small congregation can have their cake and eat it too by asking to become a part of the multisite church described in chapter 4.

5. Given the size, quality, and location of their real estate, the majority of small American Protestant congregations have four options in the building in which they now meet. One is to acquire adjacent property, expand their facilities, and enlarge their ministry in order to reach and serve more people. A second is to attempt to remain on a plateau in size. That may be a realistic goal in small-town America. A third is to attract that high-energy and visionary minister with the magnetic personality who also is a superb preacher, a loving shepherd, an inspiring teacher, and a great administrator. By expanding the weekend worship schedule to five services, worship attendance can quintuple. The problem is the current demand for these ministers exceeds the supply by a 300 to 1 ratio.

A fourth option is to relocate to a new and larger site at a better location and provide new physical facilities that enable this congregation to compete as a regional church. This is more likely to be a success story if the pastor has had at least seven years on the staff of a very large regional church that has relocated its meeting place during the past decade or two. Experience can be valuable! Twenty years after the relocation of the meeting place, it is apparent that staffing was a more influential variable than real estate in determining the success of that venture.

6. A denominational turnaround strategy does not include a strong affirmation of congregational mergers. Instead of following the traditional pattern based on the hope that

merging weakness with weakness will produce strength (4 plus 8 will equal at least 15), this strategy calls for the union of three congregations plus a compelling vision of a new day plus effective ministerial leadership.

The leaders of three congregations meet and agree to unite; one may be averaging 25 at worship, a second 35, and the third 40. Their strategy calls for disposing of all three parcels of real estate (that avoids producing two losers and one winner) and the purchase of a new site at a location that is consistent with the creation of a large regional congregation. They find a venturesome and entrepreneurial minister who has the potential for at least a twenty-year pastorate and who has at least seven years of experience on the staff of a large regional church. Five years after the first public worship service in that new location, one-third of the people who were members at the time of merger have left, but this new regional church is averaging at least 400 at worship and resembles a healthy new mission.

This discussion leads to three conclusions. First, in most cases, bringing in the minister with the required passion, vision, and skills, plus the appropriate theological stance, gifts, personality, experience, potential tenure, and priorities is the key to creating a new future for most small American Protestant congregations in today's highly competitive ecclesiastical environment. Second, there is a severe national shortage of those pastors. Third, encouraging smaller congregations to petition a large multisite church to be "adopted" as an off-campus ministry is a new and attractive option.

XVII. Utilize the Power of Television

One of the most expensive components of a turnaround strategy calls for utilizing television to invite people to church. This can be highly effective in the very large congregation with a surplus of off-street parking that is located in a relatively low-cost television market and is served by a long tenured senior minister who projects an attractive television personality. It also can be reasonably effective, although expensive, when one pastor is selected to be the symbolic minister representing that denomination. In small markets, individual congregations also may use cable television effectively. A new potential emerged in 2003 when the Comcast Corporation began to offer "zoned" advertising spots on television targeted at relatively small geographically defined areas. One thirty-second TV ad targeted at 24,000 households cost $40 while another aimed at a zone with 61,000 households was priced at $75.

Television, however, is a channel of communication that is useful for "selling" personalities. It is not effective for marketing institutions. This limits its value if the goal is to promote the popularity of a specific denominational brand name unless that message emphasizes "what our denomination opposes" in order to rally viewers against that enemy. The differences among congregations within each of the two dozen largest American denominations are greater than the differences between denominations. This point is especially significant if that denomination is engaged in a public internal quarrel over doctrine, values, and practices.

This becomes an even more difficult assignment if that denominational family also is attempting to affirm a high degree of theological pluralism and/or demographic diversity in its constituency. Television is designed for market segmentation, not for a universal appeal.

During the past few years at least $30 million has been spent by the Church of Jesus Christ of Latter-day Saints, The United Methodist Church, the Evangelical Lutheran Church in America, the United Church of Christ, and a couple of other mainline Protestant denominations on television commercials. That is the equivalent to a $100,000 subsidy for each of 300 new missions.

These are among the reasons promoting the denominational brand name via television commercials is placed so low on this list of the components for a turnaround strategy.

XVIII. Revitalizing Those Aging and Numerically Shrinking Congregations

What are the criteria that will be used in determining the priorities as you rank the various components of the turnaround strategy for your denomination? If the most influential are (1) the demand from congregational leaders, (2) the plea for "good stewardship of our resources" and (3) a desire to recreate 1955, the number one priority probably will be the renewal of aging and numerically shrinking congregations. A distant second may be a focus on planting more new missions. One reason that is second is because many congregational leaders see that as creating additional unwanted competition for future constituents.

A different criterion for ordering priorities has been used in outlining this chapter. This places equal weight on (a) difficulty, (b) costs, and (c) probability of success. That drops this component to near the end of this list. The biggest reason is cost. The critical cost is in the decisions on where to assign the most gifted transformational leaders from that inventory of parish pastors. A second reason is the difficulty of that assignment. A third is a low success rate.

A fourth, which is seldom mentioned, is in the choice of words. The two most widely used words are "revitalization" or "renewal." Both carry somewhere between neutral and positive connotations. A more realistic choice of words focuses on a term that, with one exception, normally evokes opposition. That word is "change." That exception comes when widespread agreement exists that "We are faced with a life and death crisis."

Another useful perspective to bring to this discussion is to ask a simple question. Scattered across the American ecclesiastical landscape are at least a few thousand Protestant congregations that once could be described as aging and numerically shrinking, with a limited future. In many of these, the expert's recommendation was dissolution. In others that recommendation was to become part of a multichurch parish served by one pastor or to merge with another small congregation. Today, however, that congregation has grown in numbers, is committed to fulfilling the Great Commission, and is attracting far more new constituents than it loses in the typical year. A common explanation is it has been transformed from a chaplaincy into a mission-driven community of believers.

What is the most useful umbrella term to use in describing these success stories? Most of them represent discontinuity with the past. In many the successor to the pastor who was a loving shepherd turned out to be a transformational leader. That series of relatively brief pastorates of three to ten years has been replaced by a long pastorate by that transformational leader. Typically close to one-third of the regular worshipers of that chaplaincy era departed because the level of discontinuity with the past was more than they could tolerate. The vast majority of today's most widely respected and influential volunteers are members who joined after the arrival of that transformational leader. For some the most difficult facet of discontinuity was the decision to relocate the meeting place to new facilities on a larger site at a better location.

For many the greatest discontinuity came on Sunday morning. In the old days, "I could look around and every face was that of a friend or an acquaintance. Last Sunday morning I looked around, and I realized I could not call more than 10 percent of the worshipers correctly by name. We're expected to welcome first-time visitors, but I can't tell who is a member and who may be a visitor." The discontinuity is from intimacy to anonymity.

One of the most interesting, most productive, and, for some but not all members, the most rewarding options comes when the members of that aging and numerically shrinking congregation ask to become the "North Campus" or the "Washington Avenue Campus" of that multisite church described in chapter 4. That decision usually enables the members of that small to midsized congregation to (a) continue to worship in that familiar room filled with sacred memories, (b) be inspired by sermons that combine excellent content with superb communication skills, (c) have full access to a variety of specialized ministries and programs, (d) retain a considerable degree of continuity with the past including local traditions, and (e) be assured "Our church is not a dying institution! Look at all the new people we're attracting."

What are the central themes for this component of a denominational strategy? They can be summarized in three words: discontinuity, choices, and financial subsidies. The first is to be clear that all of the options call for discontinuity with the past. The churchgoing population of twenty-first-century America includes very few forty-year-old adults born before 1930—and for many of these congregations that age cohort was the heart of that congregation's constituency in 1955.

Second, respect both the right and the power of self-determination. Help today's leaders build a list of a dozen or more possible courses of action including petitioning to join a large multisite congregation, or initiating a union with two other similar congregations to create a new future under a new name with new leadership in a new meeting place at a new location. One of these options could be outsourcing this assignment to a team or to a teaching church that specializes in congregational renewal.

Third, if your denomination has the resources to do this, offer matching financial grants if more dollars are required to implement a specific course of action. That could include replacing the current part-time pastor with a full-time minister or the relocation of the meeting place or the launching of a new specialized ministry. Those grants, however, should always be offered on a matching basis with a clearly stated terminal date. A common pattern is one dollar in subsidies for every two additional dollars contributed by members.

They also should be offered only to help create the new, not to subsidize perpetuating the old. Third, they cannot be received until after completion of a satisfactory annual performance audit. These subsidies should have a terminal date—typically a three-year maximum. They should not be allowed to degenerate into a perpetual annual subsidy.

XIX. Staff the Position of Risk Management

One of the fastest growing vocations in the American economy is for persons who specialize in risk management. One obvious reason is to minimize litigation. Lawsuits cost money! Therefore one goal is to reduce the possibilities of becoming the defendant in a lawsuit.

A bigger reason, however, is to enable people to understand identifiable or probable risks. Insurance companies are in the risk management business. Medicare is the single largest risk management component of the American economy. Another version is to calculate the risks in making either/or decisions. Hospitals and surgeons are in the risk management business. So is the person on the staff of the college or university who makes room assignments for first-year students in those school-owned residence halls. The bishop who assigns pastors to congregations is in the risk management business.

Perhaps the most highly skilled example of this specialty in American Protestantism is the legal counsel who advises denominational policy-makers on the issues related to the consequences of ascending liability. In real estate, specialists identify the risks that may accompany the purchase of a particular parcel of land. In public education, under a variety of titles, specialists identify the risks when alternative policies are being debated.

If your denomination includes more than 800 congregations, consideration should be given to employment of an experienced specialist to estimate the risks that lie between success and failure in the design of that model for planting a particular new mission, in a plan to revitalize a particular congregation, in a proposed merger of two or more congregations, in the expenditures of denominational dollars on television, in a congregation's proposal to relocate its meeting place, in the succession plans for the replacement of key staff persons in that very large congregation, in explaining the various alternatives open to the leaders in that congregation in which the average worship attendance has dropped from 350 in 1985 to 240 in 1995 to 115 last year, and in that large congregation that is choosing between sponsoring a new mission or becoming a multisite church.

If measuring potential benefits against dollar costs were the only criterion for ranking the components in this chapter, this would be placed first. One reason it is ranked so low is the probable difficulty in persuading policy-makers this would be a productive investment. A more influential reason is the national shortage of adults who possess the gifts and experience required to fill this position. A third reason is the reluctance to invest today in an action that may not produce the desired results for another three or four or five years. Building that experience base takes time!

XX. Encourage Congregational Mergers

If this chapter included thirty, rather than twenty-one possible components for a denominational turnaround strategy, this would be ranked twenty-eight, just ahead of closing churches and transforming the culture.

While exceptions do exist, the historical record suggests that in the vast majority of congregational mergers, 4 plus 6 usually equals 3 to 7, not 10 or 12. In other words, the success rate makes this a high-risk option.

One big exception, as described earlier, is when three small congregations, no one of which represents a majority of the total constituents, come together around the goal of creating a new tomorrow. All three parcels of real estate are sold. That eliminates the winner/loser problem. The compelling

145

vision is to come together to create what resembles a new mission. The design is driven by an evangelistic passion to reach, attract, serve, nurture, assimilate, and challenge a new constituency rather than to "take better care of our current membership."

If it were not for that type of exception, this option, like the option of closing churches, would not even be on this list of possible components for a denominational turnaround strategy.

XXI. Transform the Culture

The primary reason for placing this last among these twenty-one possible components of a turnaround strategy combines two social and demographic patterns. On the one hand, during the past half century the population of the United States has become increasingly diverse in terms of race, ancestry, language, religion, income, health, age, education, accumulated wealth, occupations, marital status, dress codes, transportation, housing, and other variables. On the other hand, voluntary associations tend to place a high value on homogeneity.

The reason for including the second chapter (perhaps it should have been the first?) was to identify three distinctly different types of religious bodies in the United States. At one end of this spectrum are those that were designed to be high expectation, high commitment covenant communities based on clearly defined and widely accepted legal principles that include a precisely defined doctrinal position. Two of the current examples are the Roman Catholic Church in America and the Seventh-day Adventist Church.

At the other end of that spectrum are those religious bodies that are voluntary associations of individuals, congregations, denominational agencies, and a variety of other church-related institutions such as camps, homes, theological schools, and publishing houses. They are bound together by a shared doctrinal statement, but everyone retains the right to nullify most of those legal principles as well as to exercise the right of unilateral withdrawal.

The highly visible example at this end of the spectrum consists of those congregations that are partners in an inter-church coalition. Some of these are identified as denominations, but they really are voluntary associations of autonomous congregations. Two examples at opposite ends of the theological spectrum are the Southern Baptist Convention and the Unitarian Universalist Association.

Between the religious bodies based on legal principles and the voluntary associations are most of the mainline Protestant denominations. A few, like the Episcopal Church USA and The United Methodist Church, are near one end of this spectrum while the American Baptists, the Disciples of Christ, and the United Church of Christ are near the opposite end.

If the goal is to transform the culture, how does a single religious body accomplish that? A brief detour to review six examples from American history may offer some relevant insights.

The first of these six was the antislavery movement of the nineteenth century. While the Congregationalists initially created that movement, three large evangelical Protestant bodies of that era—Methodists, Baptists, and Presbyterians—provided most of the troops for that battle. Among the consequences were schisms within each of those three denominations, nullification, secession, the Civil War, the Emancipation Proclamation, three amendments to the Constitution of the United States of America, and Reconstruction.

Overlapping that on the calendar was the Temperance Movement, which produced both allies and opponents from among the Christian denominations in the United States. That effort to transform the American culture led to the adoption of two constitutional amendments, with the second canceling the first.

A third crusade was to secure legal enforcement of the proper observance of the Christian Sabbath. This defined the workweek for adults (except for farmers, homemakers, et al.) and the school week for educational institutions. It did produce thousands of state statutes and municipal ordinances often described as "blue laws," but entertainment, gambling, recreation, and retail trade have become completely exempt in most communities.

Fourth, the Civil Rights Movement of the 1950s and 1960s produced deep divisions within several Protestant denominations, but it also led to an unprecedented alliance among Protestants, Catholics, and Jews. That single-issue alliance was shattered over a series of pelvic issues about human sexuality, including abortion, artificial birth control, the role of women, and the rights of homosexuals.

The fifth crusade was based on the historic Christian opposition to gambling. It produced more yawns than activists. At this writing twenty-nine states, including several in the South, have decided that gambling is a legitimate source of revenues for governmental budgets.

The sixth of these crusades began to gain greater visibility and many more active supporters in early 2002. This is the most recent expression of the antiwar movement. This became a big issue in the Democratic primaries in the late winter of 2003–2004 and also was a significant issue in the Presidential election of November 2004. It produced interfaith coalitions. It also produced modest internal divisions within those American religious bodies that had concluded God was calling them to engage in highly visible and divisive intradenominational quarrels over money, doctrine, human sexuality, American foreign policy, diversity, how to respond to that increasing competition for new generations of constituents, and pursuit of the charitable dollar.

One lesson from these six crusades to transform the American culture is the value of building a coalition across religious boundaries. A second is the difficulty of avoiding divisive intradenominational quarrels. A third and perhaps the most important, is to focus on a single issue and expect to create a new coalition for each issue. A fourth is to look for allies that are located about where your denomination is on that spectrum described in chapter 2. A fifth is that the greater the demographic diversity and/or theological pluralism among the constituents of any one denomination, the more difficult it may be to build an intradenominational consensus. If, however, the top priority in your denomination is on reversing years of numerical decline rather than on transforming the American culture, that raises a more difficult question.

How Do You Transform the Denominational Culture?

The historical record suggests it is more difficult to transform a denominational culture than it is to build an alliance to transform the national culture.

One success story has been the Americanization of what originally were immigrant denominational systems. The Dutch Reformed, the Swedish Baptists, the German Methodists, the Norwegian Lutherans, the German Baptists, and the Swedish Free Church are a half dozen examples. Each one has been transformed into an American religious body by enlisting allies from among future generations of American-born members, by intermarriage with other nationality groups, by exercising considerable patience, by placing a high priority on evangelism, and by honoring the past. Several have facilitated the process by denominational mergers.

What changes must be made in your denomination's culture to facilitate a reversal of those shrinking numbers? A dozen possibilities can be offered to stimulate the discussion on this issue.

First, accept the fact that a growing number of American churchgoers will drive to church while a shrinking number will walk. This raises problems in New York City, in parts of Chicago or Detroit or San Francisco and other large central cities, but that is the dominant pattern in the twenty-first century. Off-campus ministries that are a part of the total ministry of very large multisite congregations can serve the people who must or prefer to walk to church. The Key Church Strategy provides a tested model of this approach.

Second, replace the denominational culture that assumes a majority of congregations will average fewer than 100 at worship with a culture that declares the normative size is an average worship attendance of more than 500.

Third, reinforce and support the demand for accountability by mandating that annual audit of performance described in the first chapter.

Fourth, replace the denominational culture that tolerates and may even reward mediocrity with a culture driven by a passion for excellence.

Fifth, replace the culture built on low expectations of church members with a high expectation, high commitment culture. Instead of affirming a ratio of church attendance to membership of 50 or 60 or 70 percent, project an expectation that the ratio of worship attendance to membership will be at least to 2 to 1. Replace that low threshold into full membership with a high threshold designed to transform new believers into disciples and apostles.

Sixth, instead of designing staffing configurations for congregations on the assumption, "We have a scarcity of gifted pastors," design a variety of new configurations on the assumption, "We enjoy an abundance of gifted, deeply committed, and skilled laypersons." Provide meaningful, equipping events and experiences for your lay volunteers in ministry.

Seventh, replace the two-thousand-year-old temptation to choose up sides and quarrel over issues related to human sexuality with that two-thousand-year-old tradition of how Christians can create new models that can be replicated by others on how to fulfill the Great Commission.

Eighth, replace that old denominational culture that assumes the normal career path for a minister will include serving at least four or five different congregations between ordination and retirement with a culture that assumes the typical pastorate will be fifteen to forty years.

Ninth, replace the denominational culture that encourages ideological and theological pluralism with a culture driven by John 14:6 and Matthew 28:19-20.

Tenth, challenge that religious culture that assumes every sermon should be delivered personally by a live human being and replace it with a culture that affirms the delivery of that message by videotape or DVD. This already is a widely accepted concept in hundreds of congregations.

Eleventh, abandon that old religious culture that assumes three of the essential characteristics of a Christian worshiping community are (a) we are a separate and self-governing community, (b) we have one meeting place, and (c) we have our own minister. Replace it with a religious culture that assumes most congregations can and should be part of a larger system that includes two or three or three hundred different sites, but is organized around one goal, one message, either one messenger or one collegium of messengers, one governing board, one staff, one budget, and one treasury.

Finally, replace that natural preference to attempt to perpetuate the old with an understanding it often is easier to create the new than to recreate the old.

The skeptic may interpret this checklist as a dozen reasons why it is unrealistic to attempt to change the culture of any American denomination that traces its heritage back to Western Europe.

CHAPTER FOUR

THE MULTISITE OPTION

One of the widest and deepest chasms in American Protestantism divides two groups of congregational leaders from one another. The larger of the two includes those born after 1910 who believe that a useful synonym for a Christian community is "a church." That term refers to a congregation of believers who gather weekly to worship a Trinitarian God and to celebrate the birth, life, ministry, death, and resurrection of Jesus the Christ. Ideally that arrangement calls for a congregationally owned meeting place that is available for religious uses up to 168 hours every week and calls for that congregation to be served by a full-time and fully credentialed resident pastor. One of the basic assumptions is one minister can and will bring the gifts, skills, learning, experience, and wisdom required to preach effectively on all facets of the Christian Gospel.

On the other side of that deep chasm are gathered those who (a) were born before 1650, (b) were members of a Dutch Reformed Church in a place we now call New York City, (c) have retained an exceptionally high level of competence to recall events and patterns from many decades earlier, and (d) accept as a simple fact of life that no one human being could possess all the gifts, skills, learning, experience, and wisdom required to preach effectively on all facets of the Christian Gospel. The solution to this problem was for one

153

congregation to meet in several locations. That enabled the people to mobilize the resources required to be served by a team of ministers or a "collegium." This "collegiate church" was served by two or more ministers and included two or more meeting places. The preaching assignments rotated among the clergy. This past weekend Reverend A preached at location one while Reverend B delivered the message at site two, and Reverend C preached to the congregation at the third location. By rotating the ministers from place to place, the people were able to be inspired by sermons that reflected all facets of the Gospel.

One consequence is today a large group of congregational and denominational leaders are convinced that the possibility of one congregation with one name, one governing board, one ministerial staff, and one budget, and meeting at several locations is a new idea.

The natural, normal, and predictable response to what is perceived as a new idea is to reject it. That is the safe alternative. If it is a bad idea, rejection will prevent adoption. If it really is a good idea, it will surface again and again. This usually means when the multisite option is introduced as a new idea, it will be rejected.

If one introduces the multisite option as a design that has more than three centuries of experience behind it in American Christianity, the response may be, "How did they do it? What can we learn from them that will be of value to us today?" "How can we improve on that design given the fact we have access to technology not available to American Christians in the seventeenth and eighteenth centuries?"

This book discusses twenty-one different components as possibilities for inclusion in a denominational turnaround strategy. Which ranks up there with planting new missions as among the oldest? Which one has the highest success rate? Which one ranks among the five easiest to implement? Which one draws most heavily on the creativity, the commitments, the gifts, the skills, the enthusiasm, and the cooperation of lay volunteers? Which component ranks among the three most promising alternatives for producing a dramatic turnaround in that aging small congregation with a dwindling membership? Which one ranks among the three alternatives requiring only a modest or no continuing financial subsidy from the denominational treasury? Which ranks among the three most promising in producing a substantial return on the investment of resources? Which provides the most satisfying response to the issue of the future of the small congregation versus the megachurch? Which of these twenty-one alternatives is least dependent on that limited supply of exceptionally gifted ministers who are both entrepreneurial leaders and excellent preachers? Which of these alternatives tops the list in terms of the use of modern technology?

From this traveler's perspective the answer to all ten of those questions is the multisite option.[1] If that is true, why is it ranked tenth rather than first back in chapter 3? The answer is that set of ten questions overlooked three other criteria.

Which of those twenty-one alternatives represents the greatest departure from twentieth-century traditions? Which of these alternatives is most vulnerable to the allegation, "All they're doing over there is building up their own religious empire"? Which of these twenty-one alternatives represents the greatest threat to a long list of sacred institutions and practices such as the geographically defined parish church, the regulatory authority of denominational systems, the future of theological seminaries, the authority of the clergy, the role of traditional denominational budgeting systems, the power of inherited denominational loyalty, the practice of sermons being delivered in person by a live preacher, the role of the ordained generalist, the relationships of each worshiping community to its denominational system, the geographical relationships of the place of worship to the worshipers' places of residence, and the power of the homogeneous unit principle in church growth?

The answer to that set of criteria also is the multisite option. It should rank first because of its effectiveness. It ranks tenth because it is so difficult to win denominational approval for such a radical departure from "How we've always done church."

It also ranks tenth, and some would drop it to twenty-second place in this list of twenty-one scenarios, because it affirms intradenominational competition among congregations for future constituents. The conventional wisdom suggests congregations should not compete with one another for future constituents. In real life, they do. A common example is the congregation meeting in a building in a village with a population of 600. John and Mary Brown both are third-generation members. Both were born in the 1930s. Both are among the most loyal members of this congregation that now averages 95 at worship. Their son, Allen, married a wife, Laura, who was reared in another denomination a hundred miles away. Allen inherited the family business. Allen, Laura, and their two teenage children commute fourteen miles each way to a large church of the same denomination as Allen was reared in years ago. One explanation is a more extensive youth ministry. A second is better preaching. A third is Laura prefers not to be identified as "John Brown's daughter-in-law." A fourth reason is the far larger number of mothers of Laura's generation.

Another example may be the denominational merger that produced two congregations that now have the same denominational affiliation and worship in buildings across the street from one another.

One consequence of this opposition to the multisite option is a disproportionately large number of the most creative models has been produced by nondenominational congregations or in traditions that encourage local initiative, such as the Southern Baptist Convention, and that focus on fulfilling the Great Commission.

Does This Belong on Your List?

Given the positive characteristics of the multisite option, could your denomination adopt and implement it? If your denomination places a very high priority on evangelism, the answer is clearly in the affirmative. The Key Church Strategy has been a remarkably effective and well-received effort among Southern Baptists. That strategy fits under the generic label of a multisite ministry. [2]

If, however, a higher priority in your denominational system is placed on expanding intradenominational quarreling over doctrine, human sexuality, American foreign policy, ecumenism, funding denominational entitlements, reducing the number of congregations, or financial subsidies, you may want to skip this chapter. Adoption and implementation could threaten those who are committed to perpetuating old traditions or who believe every congregation should serve a geographically defined constituency. This could add more fuel to the fires of intradenominational quarreling!

Multisite congregations come in a variety of shapes, sizes, and patterns, but most represent one of three basic approaches.

Create the New

The most common approach is when a single-site congregation unilaterally decides to become a two-site ministry. A common example is the congregation meeting in what is now a functionally obsolete building on an inadequate site at what has become a poor location. The Long Range Planning Committee recommends relocation. At the congregational meeting the vote is 57 percent in favor of relocation and 43 percent opposed. The opposition includes several influential long-tenured members.

The compromise is to answer that question, "Should we relocate or stay here?" with a resounding, "Yes!" A new site is purchased, the first unit of the proposed three-stage building program is constructed, and the program staff is expanded. The result is a two-site congregation.

Another contemporary version frames the question in different terms. "Should we send money to our denomination to help finance a new mission on the west side of town or should we become a two-site church?" A review of the historical record reveals that of the last seven new missions planted by this denomination in this region or conference, two closed within five years, four have plateaued in size with worship attendance averaging fewer than 135, and one now averages 360 at worship in its sixth year of existence.

A volunteer leader at what had been asked to be a sponsoring congregation suggests, "We can raise the $200,000 that is our share for this mission without any problem, but I don't believe that is the number one resource that is needed. During the past eight years our average worship attendance has nearly doubled from about 450 to close to 900. We have learned how to reach, attract, and assimilate hundreds of newcomers. I believe our biggest contribution to a new church for our denomination on the west side would be if we could export what we have learned about how to do big church in this community in the twenty-first century. The question is, how do we do that?"

Two months later that question has been answered. The best way to produce that export is to become a two-site ministry. Land is purchased for what is referred to as "our west campus," and the money is raised to pay for the land and for construction of the first unit of the building program. (A related version calls for purchase of an existing building on a site that represents a good location for the west campus.)

Instead of designing and staffing a new model for church planting, the decision is to rely on the experience and staff, both paid and volunteer, of a model that has been successful in reaching new constituents in this general community. The culture, passion, skills, experiences, learning, and creativity of an effective working model is more valuable as an "export" than is money.

A variation of this same model that emphasizes exporting the resources of the large congregation is based on four assumptions. First, instead of inviting people to come and worship God with us in our big, intimidating building, our call in the Great Commission is to carry the Gospel of Jesus Christ to people where they are. Second, barriers such as language, social class, skin color, nationality, and education are real. While it is not ideologically popular, the homogeneous unit principle does describe reality. Most residents of the United States prefer to be with people "who are like me." That is the nature of most voluntary associations.

Third, the natural, normal, and comfortable size for a worshiping community in the Christian faith is an average attendance of fewer than forty.[3] In American Protestantism one out of every seven congregations report their worship attendance averages 25 or fewer. That also explains why house churches should be considered as one component of a turnaround strategy.

What is one of the most significant differences between the congregation in American Protestantism that averages 85 at worship and the one that averages 850? Both rank in the larger half in size among all Protestant churches in the United States, but in the smaller ones, the most deeply committed and gifted lay volunteers tend to be asked to be engaged in administration. In the very large congregations the vast majority of those committed and gifted lay volunteers are challenged to be engaged in doing ministry. That introduces the fourth assumption. How do we raise the money to pay more program staff? We don't do that! We staff our off-campus ministries with committed, gifted, and equipped teams of lay volunteers and part-time paid specialists. One team of three organizes a new off-campus worshiping community in a mobile-home park. Another team builds a ministry with single-parent mothers in an apartment complex. A third team launches a new ministry with residents of housing for graduate students at the university. A fourth team creates a new ministry with residents of a large building designed for assisted living. A fifth team opens a new ministry in a storefront in the inner city.

All three of these examples of multisite congregations reflect four important themes. One is to build on strength and relevant experience, rather than on inexperience and/or failure. A second is it usually is easier to create the new at a new location than to add the new at the central site. Third, and most important, if the goal is to reach a completely new constituency, it is much easier and more effective to invite them to help pioneer the new at a new site than to create it on what appears to be someone else's turf. The fourth theme is an expanded role for lay volunteers in doing ministry. The responsibility for initiating that new ministry, for designing the model, for mobilizing the resources, for setting priorities, for enlisting and equipping additional volunteers, and for making the initial decisions rests on a team that includes both paid staff and lay volunteers.

Adopt Those Who Want Help

This judicatory includes dozens of congregations that average fewer than 75 at worship. None of them are financially able to attract, challenge, and retain the services of a full-time seminary-trained pastor. Several of them meet in good to excellent physical facilities on adequate sites at good locations but have been unable to attract the people required to replace those who die or move away or drop out. This judicatory also may include one or two new missions launched years earlier that have plateaued in size with only a few score loyal constituents.

One common response is to urge two or three of these small congregations to merge in the hope that combining weakness with weakness will produce strength. The historical record, however, suggests that in congregational mergers, like denominational mergers, 4 plus 4 rarely equals 8. What happens when the Protestant congregation averaging 40 at worship merges with another small church averaging 35 at worship? More often than not, five years later the merged congregation will be averaging somewhere between 30 and 55 at worship.

A more productive alternative is based on the assumption that bringing together limited resources with strength can produce progress. That small congregation asks that large church averaging 500 to 2,500 at worship to adopt it as the South Campus or the Jefferson Street campus or as the Loganville campus of that multisite church.[4]

The midlevel judicatory can facilitate this process by (a) challenging three or four very large congregations with the necessary discretionary resources to accept the role as a multisite missionary church and (b) in meeting with leaders of small congregations adding this to the list of seven to twenty alternative scenarios as they discuss the future of that particular congregation.

WARNING! One relevant bit of wisdom comes out of the field of adult education. "You can't teach an adult anything that adult does not want to learn!" The translation for this discussion is the influential and respected leaders in the small church must initiate the discussions with the large missionary congregation. Each adoption should be treated as a unique opportunity. That means no one can anticipate all the questions and conflicts that may arise. Therefore a common approach is to enter into a one-year or two-year agreement that cannot be extended unless both parties agree to an extension. It may mean, for example, that the small congregation will operate with its own system of governance and its own budget and will carry complete responsibility for maintenance of the real estate for that initial probationary period. The small church makes a monthly or quarterly payment to that missionary church toward the cost of shared paid staff.

After that courtship period has been completed, the door is opened to the possibility of gradually moving toward becoming one congregation with two or more sites, but with one budget, one system of governance, and one staff, and with the title to all real estate in the name of that missionary church. The crucial variable is transferring the title to the real estate to the missionary church. That "seals the deal."

An overlapping scenario fits those congregations that have been experiencing numerical decline for many years. A congregational meeting is called to vote on three questions. The first is a motion to dissolve. If that is approved, the second motion is to become the XYZ campus of that missionary church. If that is approved, the third motion is to transfer title to all assets to the missionary church. That motion may be amended to offer to return to the donor families certain items such as furniture, pictures, hymnals, or worship equipment.

Can We Have Our Cake and Eat It Too?

Literally thousands of small congregations in American Christianity want to retain their independence and continue to gather to worship God in that place filled with sacred memories, but they are unable to find a clergyperson to lead that Sunday morning worship service. At the November 2003 semiannual U.S. Conference of Catholic Bishops this issue dominated the agenda. "Sunday Celebrations in Absence of a Priest" evoked deep concern over the possible outcomes of allowing a layman or a laywoman to officiate. (Current church law prohibits a Catholic priest from presiding at more than three Masses on any one Sunday.) These services usually include the distribution of the previously consecrated hosts plus prayers, Scripture readings, and a homily. One bishop expressed concern that parishioners will depart affirming that "Mrs. Garibaldi had a nice Mass today."[5]

Small Protestant congregations have utilized dozens of different approaches to providing ministerial leadership. That long list includes (1) relying on lay volunteers to staff all roles often filled by paid staff, (2) using income from an endowment fund to balance the budget, (3) receiving a continuing denominational subsidy that enables the congregation to have a paid minister, (4) arranging for a college or seminary student to serve as the weekend preacher (this is consistent with an ideological commitment to the efficacy of short pastorates and/or the conviction that small churches represent the wave of the future for that denomination), (5) selling real estate to "tide us over until our attendance begins to climb," (6) employing a retired minister to serve as the part-time pastor (this often has great appeal to the congregation composed largely of adults born before 1940), (7) sharing a full-time and fully credentialed pastor with another small church in the same denomination (this is consistent with a long-range strategy to encourage congregational mergers), (8) sharing a pastor with another small church of a different denomination (this is consistent with the long-term goal of merging those two or three denominations), (9) providing a postseminary apprenticeship for new graduates (this is consistent with the conviction that the first pastorate out of seminary should equip graduates to serve as loving shepherds of small congregations rather than begin an apprenticeship that models the role of the pastor as an initiating leader), (10) calling a part-time licensed lay pastor (this may turn a part-time job into a full-time assignment as the congregation gradually grows in size and complexity), (11) seeking the ordained homemaker married to a spouse with a full-time job as part-time pastor (this can provide huge benefits in economic terms in housing costs and health insurance plus the potential of long tenure—the downside is where do you find a successor at that compensation level when that day eventually arrives?), (12) finding a fully credentialed minister who prefers a part-time assignment in order to have time to write or play golf or fish or go to graduate school or hunt or lead workshops and who is married to a spouse with an excellent income, (13) inviting an immigrant pastor who needs an income, a house, and time to perfect his or her skills in the English language, (14) selling the church property, leasing it back, investing the sale price and using the income from that investment to balance the budget, (15) operating a financially self-supporting ministry, such as a Christian day school or a weekday child care center or an early development center for very young children or an adult day care program, with the pastor serving as the paid director of that ministry as well as the part-time minister for that congregation, (16) opening the door to a new option when that long-tenured pastor dies and the congregation asks his mature widow, who for years had been the volunteer "assistant pastor," to become the full-time minister, and she is able to accept a lower level of compensation since she receives Social Security checks every month plus a widow's pension from her late husband's ministerial pension plan, while the denomination licenses her as a lay pastor, and/or (17) turning to the chaplain at the local nursing home or hospital or to the ordained college or seminary professor with a seminary degree to serve as the weekend preacher for this small congregation.

That long list is included here for two reasons. First, it identifies several of the alternatives open to small congregations as they design a customized ministry plan for the future. Second, and more important, all seventeen of those alternatives share a common characteristic. Each one can be a useful component of a larger strategy designed to perpetuate the status quo for a few more years. None, however, are promising options for a customized ministry plan that includes an expectation the congregation can and should double or triple or quadruple in size during the next ten years. That limitation explains why one more option should be added to the list of alternative futures for most congregations averaging fewer than a hundred at worship.

What is the most effective strategy to be followed by the congregation that has averaged fewer than a hundred at worship for decades? One answer is to change the congregational culture! What is the best way to change that culture? Perhaps the most effective way is to build in continuity with the past by continuing to gather for the corporate worship of God in that room filled with sacred memories, but be affiliated as the Oak Hill or Washington Street campus with a very large multisite congregation that is inventing and modeling how to do church in the twenty-first century in this region with residents born after 1960. Continuity with the past is carried in the real estate and by dozens of familiar faces, but that team of volunteers gradually introduces the refinements in the culture required to create a new tomorrow with new generations. This affiliate model enables everyone, old and new, to have full access to the variety of ministries and programs offered at the central location, but continue to enjoy the intimacy and the absence of complexity that are hallmarks of the small Protestant congregation in America.[6]

In many urban communities this model also enables a congregation to affirm that desire for ethnic separation in worship and learning opportunities concurrently with becoming an ethnically integrated larger fellowship. Each person at each of these monocultural meeting places can move toward ethnic integration at the pace he or she finds to be comfortable.

Finally, a significant fringe benefit in increasing the number and variety of large multisite churches can be to expand the role of your denominationally affiliated teaching churches. Instead of congregations affiliated with your denomination turning to churches of other traditions as they seek to learn how to reach and serve new generations in a new century, they can benefit from the experiences and learnings of creative teaching churches in your tradition.

One Messenger or a Collegium?

One of the crucial forks in the road in creating a multisite ministry surfaces when the decision is made on who will deliver the message at those worship experiences. One alternative is the collegium. The preaching team consists of two to five individuals. They may follow that Dutch Reformed tradition of rotating from place to place every week or two.

Modern technology, however, has created another option. All those worshiping communities receive the same message delivered by the same messenger. Twelve of those may be delivered by projected visual imagery, and two may receive that same message delivered in person. A variation calls for a live messenger at two or three or four sites at the same hour every weekend and videotape or DVD at all other services. That may require two or three live messengers with one providing the videotape for all services relying on projected visual imagery.

The reliance on the same message each weekend delivered by the same messenger does create a hazard. What happens if and when that fifty-seven-year-old minister, who has been the only messenger for the past decade or longer, looks the wrong way while crossing the street and is run over by a big truck? Life goes on. There is a period for grieving over this sudden loss. At every site, however, much of the continuity is that campus pastor who continues to serve and lead as "the face on this place." The Ministry Director continues to oversee the total ministry. The same Executive Pastor continues to supervise the administration of that large and complicated multisite ministry. The Pastoral Team continues to provide for the pastoral care of the constituents. The trustees continue to worry about the real estate. The inventory of 500 or more videotapes enables that deceased messenger to deliver a message appropriate for that season of the Christian year at every worship experience. Thanks to modern technology, just because a person is dead doesn't mean that person is gone!

After a few months of shared grieving, guest ministers, and/or other staff members deliver the message on most weekends. A year or so later that apparent vacancy becomes real, and the search begins for a permanent successor.

One advantage of the one-messenger alternative is the same person delivers the same message at every worship service, even when that messenger is on vacation in Italy or Montana or Scotland.

A second advantage is a consequence of the diminishing loyalty to institutions in the American culture. The baseball fan's primary loyalty may be to a star player rather than to that player's team. The graduate student's primary loyalty may be to a particular professor, rather than to that university. The patient's primary loyalty may be to a physician rather than to the medical clinic that employs that doctor. The parishioner's number one loyalty may be to the founding pastor of that new mission organized two decades ago, rather than to the denomination or to the congregation.

Add to that pattern a characteristic of communication in large and complex organizations. For many recipients of that communication the messenger has become the message. That was illustrated by Franklin D. Roosevelt, Ronald Reagan, and William Jefferson Clinton as Presidents of the United States. It also has been and is being illustrated by dozens of long-tenured preachers in American Protestantism. In addition, in many megachurches the continuity is in the person, the priorities, and the personality of a long-tenured senior minister.

Those are among the arguments for one messenger. Another is the culture of American Protestantism tends to affirm the single messenger rather than a collegium. Until recently theological schools trained students for the role of "the pastor," not to be members of an egalitarian team.

On the other side of this debate are several persuasive reasons for building a collegium or team. One is the demand for specialists, not generalists. A second is to offer people choices. A third is many of the clergy born after 1960 tend to be more comfortable as team players rather than as soloists. A fourth is in the fact five heads usually contain more wisdom than can be found in any one head. A fifth is no one person can relate effectively to everyone and the most treasured relationships today are more likely to be with individuals than with someone because of that person's office, title, or position. The *big* argument for the collegium, however, is what happens when the head honcho departs? How large is the resulting hole? When one member of that five-person team leaves, the resulting vacuum is much smaller than when

167

the soloist departs. Overlapping that is one other factor. When the senior minister is replaced by a new senior minister, who socializes the successor into that role? The program staff may quarrel over who should be the number one adviser to this newcomer. Or the volunteer leadership may compete for that influential assignment.

What happens when the team leader of a five-person team leaves? Who socializes that successor into "our system"? First, one of the four remaining team members may become the team leader. It is not necessary for the new preacher also to be the team leader. Second, if a newcomer fills that vacancy, the other four members of the team socialize the newcomer into "how we do church here."

Four Lines of Demarcation

This decision on a choice between one messenger and a collegium of messengers is becoming one of the most significant lines of demarcation that distinguish one type of multi-site church from others. A second is the distinction between planting new worshiping communities at off-campus sites or adopting or affiliating with existing churches. A third is in size. One pattern consists of one very large and self-identified missionary church at one location with a large number of relatively small worshiping communities, usually largely staffed by volunteers, at ten to two hundred locations. A fourth and radically different version emerges when that missionary church creates, or adopts, what become large congregations at each of several sites. Fifteen years after accepting that role as a multisite church, worship attendance may average 800 at the "home base," 1,200 at another location, 600 at a third, and 1,800 at a fourth. In today's world, many adults have children who are taller than either parent.

CHAPTER FIVE

PLANT NEW MISSIONS

You move your place of residence several hundred miles. Eventually you decide the time has come to identify the person who will serve as your primary care physician. You make your first appointment and request a physical examination. You come prepared to ask four questions. At the end of your appointment, you have asked your four questions plus two that had not occurred to you before. That physician, however, has addressed two dozen questions to you. Do you smoke? Drink? Exercise? Occupation? Marital status? Previous surgery? How long have you had that cough? Has your blood pressure always been this high? Does it hurt when I do this to your body?

For those who were born after 1950 the oral tradition of our denomination tells us two important facts. First, back in the post–World War II era when we were organizing lots of new churches, our denomination was experiencing numerical growth. Second, ever since we began to cut back on new church development, our denomination has been experiencing a numerical decline.

The obvious conclusion is the first step in designing a turnaround strategy for our denomination is to replicate the 1950s and plant lots of new missions. That reduces the agenda to four or five questions.

1. How many new missions?
2. Where do we plant them?
3. How do we pay for them?
4. Where do we find the mission-developer pastor?
5. (Optional) Who will administer this effort?

The Historical Context

A larger perspective can be provided by expanding the time frame. The peak era for new church development in the history of American Christianity came in the 1880–1906 era when at least 100,000 new congregations were organized.[1] Nearly 11,000 were affiliated with the Southern Baptist Convention. Approximately 20,000 were organized by the six predecessors of what today is The United Methodist Church. Another 7,500 were organized by the two dozen Lutheran bodies in the United States while more than 6,200 were organized by Presbyterians and nearly 6,000 by Roman Catholics. Nearly 3,400 were planted by the Northern Baptist Convention, approximately 5,500 by the Disciples of Christ, close to 4,000 by the four predecessor bodies of what today is the United Church of Christ, and 1,500 by the Seventh-day Adventists. At least 4,000 were affiliated with the National Baptist Convention and another 4,000 identified with the six black Methodist denominations. Approximately 3,000 new missions were organized by the Protestant Episcopal Church. At least 2,000 were affiliated with the Churches of Christ while approximately 500 were launched by the Reformed Church in America and 125 by the Christian Reformed Church.

While it was almost certainly an undercount, only 850 independent or nondenominational congregations reported they were organized during those twenty-seven years.

That wave of new church development was dominated by the predecessors of what today are a dozen Christian bodies. The primary constituencies consisted of five overlapping groups, (a) recent immigrants from Western Europe, (b) new-comers to that westward moving frontier, (c) freed slaves, their children, and grandchildren, (d) Americans moving from rural to urban areas, and (e) migrants from the large central cities to newly developing residential communities on the periphery.

A second big wave of new church development followed the end of World War II. A rough estimate is that an average of approximately 3,000 new congregations were planted each year in the 1946–1959 era that were still in existence in the mid-1960s. An unknown number had been launched but no longer existed in 1960.

Relatively few independent congregations trace their origins back before 1960. Three of the big exceptions to that generalization are Ohio, California, and Oklahoma. The states that experienced the largest number of new Protestant congregations during those fourteen years were California, Texas, Pennsylvania, Florida, North Carolina, Michigan, New York, and Virginia. The new church development boom in Georgia, the Pacific Northwest, and Arizona did not begin until the 1960s.

The accompanying table depicts the average number of new churches launched each year by fifteen denominations for those fourteen years from 1946 through 1959.[2] (In a few cases incomplete data has required a rounding of the numbers or represents a rough estimate.) In several, the current postmerger name of the denomination is used and the annual average is for the combined total of the predecessor denominations. In five cases the number of years covered by the reporting ranged between nine and eleven. (That annual average is for the years covered by that particular report.)

For several of these denominations this post–World War II era represented their peak years in new church development between 1928 and 2000. If a similar table were prepared for American Protestantism covering the 1970–2000 era, the top line would represent the annual average number of new non-denominational Protestant congregations and the second line would report the average number of new Southern Baptist congregations planted each year. Most of today's mainline Protestant denominations would not be among the top ten on that table. One explanation is that in four cases, denominational mergers have pushed new church development to a lower place on the agenda of denominational priorities. In at least four denominations a new sport called "Intradenominational Quarreling" has moved ahead of new church development in attracting active followers.

Table 2: Annual Average Number of New Congregations in the 1946–1959 Era	
Denomination	*Congregations*
Southern Baptist Convention	445
Assemblies of God	215
Church of the Nazarene	162
United Methodist Church	150
Ev. Lutheran Church in Am.	115
Lutheran Church-Mo. Synod	101
Episcopal Church	84
Presbyterian Church (USA)*	74
Church of God (Anderson)	52
Disciples of Christ	46
United Church of Christ	23
Christian Reformed Church	12
Church of the Brethren	10
Wisc. Ev. Lutheran Synod	10
Reformed Church in America	3

*Does not include new missions organized by the Presbyterian Church in the United States in the 1946–1959 era.

Most of the constituents for that post–World War II wave of new church development consisted of four overlapping categories: (a) veterans returning from the war, (b) persons reared in rural America who were moving to metropolitan counties, (c) residents of the central cities moving to suburbia, or (d) urbanites seeking a new church home following a move to a new address. Those four groups can be compressed into one—Americans born in the 1915–1955 era who were moving to a new address in metropolitan America. The big and highly visible exception to that sentence consisted of the new congregations in the large central cities founded to serve American-born black residents.

The Changing Context

A completely different approach to designing this component of a turnaround strategy begins with a dozen observations about the 1950s and 1960s. First, most of those new congregations launched in 1955 were designed to reach and serve (a) adults born in the 1910–1935 era and (b) their children. That was a large and underserved market that included nearly 60 million adults in 1955. By 2005, however, the number of residents of the United States who had been born in that 1910–1935 era had dropped to 26 million—and that total includes several million immigrants who came to the United States after 1960.

Second, the expectations the generations born after 1945 bring to church are more numerous, more varied, more demanding, and more expensive. One example is a conveniently located and vacant off-street parking space. A second is a gymnasium. A third is a choice in coffee. A fourth is more visual communication and less reliance on oral communication or the printed word. (Remember the racks for hymnals in the pew in front of where you sat back in the 1980s?) A fifth is air-conditioned meeting rooms. A sixth is that expansion of weekday ministries.

173

The differences among the individuals born after 1960 are far greater than the differences among Americans born in the 1910–1940 era. Individualism is a product of affluence. One consequence is the differences among the clergy are far greater today than was true in 1935 or 1955. Another is the differences among the congregations within any one of the dozen largest denominations in American Protestantism are greater than the differences between any two of those dozen denominations.

One explanation is in the differences among American Christians born after 1960. A second is the differences among theological schools. A third is the increase in the number of ministers who were educated in a college and/or the theological seminary not affiliated with their denomination. A fourth explanation is the merger of denominations coming from differing cultures or polities. A fifth is the differences among congregations in size, values, goals, priorities, and specialties.

Among the many consequences of these differences are three that affect the numerical growth or decline of a denomination. The most obvious is the increased difficulty in creating an ideal match between the needs of a congregation and the gifts, skills, personality, passions, priorities, age, theological stance, marital status, education, social class, and experience of the minister. A second is the shift from a regional to a national marketplace as congregations search for a new pastor. A third is the larger the size of a congregation, the more likely the search for a new ordained staff member will focus on candidates who have had several years of experience on the staff of a very large church.

In other words, it is more difficult to find the ideal candidate to plant a new mission today than it was in 1955 or 1975!

A third observation is in the 1950s we defined the primary constituency for a proposed new mission by their place of residence. Today we define it by the needs of the people we identify as our primary constituency.

Fourth, the contemporary competition among Christian congregations and among denominations for potential future constituents is far greater than it was fifty years ago.

Fifth, five decades ago an influential factor in the planning for new missions was the assumption that denominational loyalties tended to be inherited by each new generation from their parents. The one big exception was when a Roman Catholic married a Protestant. In four out of five of those marriages, the operational assumption was the Protestant spouse would convert to Catholicism.

Today denominational loyalties are far weaker. The new mission that averages 500 at worship after two years may report 15 percent of the constituents previously were affiliated with that denomination, 20 percent were reared in a Roman Catholic family, 25 percent were actively involved in a Protestant church not affiliated with this denomination, and 40 percent had no active church affiliation before joining this new mission.

Sixth, a widely followed design called for a pastor to bring together 25 to 75 adults as the nucleus for a new congregation. From that tiny acorn eventually a mighty oak would grow. A far more frequent outcome was that within a decade that new mission would (a) plateau in size with an average worship attendance of fewer than 125 or (b) dissolve or (c) merge with another congregation, and sometimes that would be the sponsoring church. Today a common goal is for that new mission to be averaging at least 500 at worship within five years of the first public worship services.

Seventh, the cost per acre of land for a new mission, or for expanding the site of a congregation organized many decades earlier, has increased dramatically. In 1955, for example, sites for new churches often were priced at $1,000 to $3,000 per acre. Thus a three-acre site could be purchased for $3,000 to $10,000. That figure varied depending on whether the property had been improved with paved streets plus sewer and water lines. Today the cost per acre for a new church site is

175

more likely to be in the $10,000 to $300,000 range. It is not unusual for a city church to pay in the range of $1 million to $3 million per acre to expand a site originally acquired in 1885 or 1925 or 1955.

Another example is the neighborhood congregation founded in 1950 that purchased two acres for its meeting place. Fifty years later the members decide to relocate in order to become a large regional church. They pay $1.2 million for that sixty-acre relocation site and rejoice that it was available at that price.

Eighth, one of the most significant changes is the answer to that question, "How much land will we need?" In 1885 one answer was two or three residential lots. A second was an acre of land. A third was two acres, an acre for the church and an acre for the cemetery.

By 1955 the standard recommendation was three acres. One acre for parking for 100 to 125 cars, another acre for the building, and an acre for setbacks and landscaping. Hundreds of sites for new missions, however, were purchased that were less than three acres.

Today the standard recommendation is at least ten usable acres, but future-oriented leaders are purchasing sites in the 40- to 300-acre range. Scores of congregations that either are (a) relocating their ministries to a new location or (b) in the process of becoming multisite churches consider 40 acres to be the minimum.

The master plan for what is expected to become a "destination" type congregation averaging at least 4,500 at weekend worship may allocate 30 to 40 acres for setbacks, open space, storm water control, and landscaping, 20 acres for parking, 10 acres for interior streets, 60 acres for a retirement village, 20 acres for recreation, 10 acres for a Christian day school for ages 3 to 12, perhaps 5 acres for a retreat center, and 35 acres for buildings to house a variety of other ministries. These "ministry villages" or "destination" type congregations are based on what may be the most significant single change in church planning since the 1950s.

Ninth, the journey to work, to shopping, to entertainment, to recreation, to "our summer home," to school, and to church is longer. One highly visible example was the eighteen-year-old who "went away to school" following high school graduation and lived in a dormitory. Today hundreds of thousands of young adults live at home and commute five to thirty miles daily to classes. The walk from the dorm to the classroom has been replaced by the student parking permit. For seventeen-year-olds that transition may begin earlier in life with the four-mile drive from home to the student parking lot at the local public high school.

After years of practice in driving to school, to recreation, to entertainment, to work, to the mall, and to visit friends, it is easy to master the skill of driving ten or twenty or thirty miles to church. The neighborhood congregation of 1955 was beginning to be replaced in the 1970s by the large regional church that served a constituency living within a ten-mile radius of the meeting place. The new kid on the block is the destination congregation that serves hundreds of members who walk to church from that retirement village plus a few thousand who drive two to thirty miles to church in their own motor vehicles.

That introduces the tenth and eleventh of these changes that can be summarized in the question, "Why?" One answer to that question is described as "Per Capita Disposable Personal Income." After allowing for inflation, the average per capita disposable personal income in the United States nearly quadrupled between 1955 and 2005. Most Americans now can afford what once was described as a luxury—the cost of private personal transportation to the destination of one's choice. That also means the members can afford the cost of a larger site, a more luxurious meeting place, and a greater variety of ministries. One highly visible consequence is the need for a far larger parking lot. The old standard of one off-street parking space for every four seats in the largest room in the building has been replaced by a demand for 100

177

off-street parking spaces for every 200 people at worship on the average Sunday morning—and that is the combined attendance for all Sunday morning services.

The next to last of these dozen changes is illustrated most clearly by major league football and baseball teams. The demand is for a higher level of performance. One consequence is more specialists and fewer generalists. Instead of expecting a member of the backfield to accept the responsibility for punting and placekicking, the team hires two specialists. Only rarely is a professional football player expected to play on both the offensive and defensive teams. The American League baseball teams now carry a designated hitter, a gifted substitute outfielder, a reserve defensive infielder, three or four "setup" relief pitchers, and a closer on the roster.

In 1885 an evangelistic preacher was asked to start a new congregation. In 1955 an ordained generalist received that assignment. Today that team of three to nine persons (a couple of whom may be part-time or volunteers) who go out to plant a new mission usually consists of specialists. Each one carries one or two basic responsibilities. That list might include the visionary leader, a specialist in communicating the Gospel of Jesus Christ, the builder of learning communities, a spiritual mentor, the executive pastor who is responsible for a smooth-running institution with internally consistent and compatible goals, the worship team leader, an expert in creative use of projected visual imagery, an evangelist, a specialist in equipping the laity for ministry, a minister of missions, and a specialist in ministries with families with children at home. If three full-time persons each carry two specialized responsibilities and four part-time persons each carry one, that initial goal of averaging a thousand at worship one year after the first public worship service becomes attainable.

Other staff configurations for a new mission might include a specialist in ministries with teenagers or a public relations expert or a parish nurse or a specialist in young adult ministries or a specialist in community ministries.

Finally, the most controversial change in the contemporary
context for ministry is one that often generates cries of
"Heresy!" or evokes passionate hostility. In the good old
days of the 1950s, football was a sport, television and radio
presented reports of the news of the day, teachers taught the
subject they were assigned to teach, preachers delivered
inspirational sermons, parishioners dressed in their Sunday
best to go to church, restaurants served meals to hungry customers, automobile manufacturers produced vehicles for
transportation, the commercial airlines hired registered
nurses to provide passenger services, and purchasing goods
at a retail store was something between a duty and a chore.
Church membership carried obligations, one of which was to
come and listen to every word of the sermon. Another was to
accept and obey church law. The improvement of social skills
was a central goal of various activities for children called
"play."

Today professional football is designed to entertain huge
crowds. That three- or four-person team anchoring the local
news on television is chosen to represent diversity in terms of
ethnicity and gender. Their assignment is to present the news
wrapped in a package of entertainment. One of the criteria
used by students to evaluate both high school and university
teachers is their competence in grabbing and holding the
attention of teenagers and young adults. The dress code in
most American Protestant congregations has been relaxed,
and the clothing one would wear to the playground is acceptable for church. One responsibility of flight attendants is to
entertain the passengers. The candidates for elective political
office who wear a perpetual smile and are entertaining public speakers have a big edge over their rivals who rarely smile
and have never mastered the skill of telling a joke in which
they are the butt of the punch line. Motor vehicles are
designed and sold as toys for recreation as well as for travel
rather than for economy of operation. Restaurants are
judged on the basis of service, food, and ambiance. Shopping

often is described as either a hobby or as entertainment. A magic toy processes the desired software called computer games to provide solitary entertainment for children and teenagers. The preachers who accept the obligation to grab and hold the attention of worshipers are either criticized or admired for their skills as stand-up comedians who also provide the continuity for a series of brief visual images periodically projected on a screen.

In today's living rooms, classrooms, worship centers, shopping malls, family rooms, sports stadiums, motion picture theaters, political campaigns for elective offices, and churches, information comes wrapped in entertainment.

The response of many born after 1965 is, "That's the way its been for as long as I can remember." The response of a larger proportion of those born before 1955 is, "That's really not the way God intended it to be." The question for those designing the turnaround strategy for your denomination is, "Do you believe 2010 will resemble 1955 or will it resemble 2005?" Should your planning be driven by a desire to replicate 1955 or by the challenge to help create a new tomorrow for your denomination?

The Fourth Great Awakening

It could be argued that the most useful context for designing a denominational strategy for new church development begins with the question, What year is it? If the answer is 2005, 2006, or 2007, that translates into the fifth decade of the fourth big religious revival in American history.[3] There may be some dispute over whether it began in 1960 or 1965, but there is no question but that an unprecedented number of Americans are on a self-identified religious quest. The highly visible evidences of this include the record enrollment in more than a hundred "Christ-centered" Christian colleges and universities, the emergence of "seeker-sensitive" megachurches overflowing with constituents born after

1950, the articles devoted to this trend in the secular news-magazines, the demand for resources, experiences, and events that are designed to help individuals on a self-described spiritual journey, the migration of faithful church-goers from Roman Catholic and mainline Protestant congregations to evangelical churches, the essays by self-identified nonbelievers on the impact of this religious reawakening,[4] the role of religion in the 2004 political campaigns for the presidency of the United States, the attention the public opinion polls have given to this trend in recent years, and the attendance in Bible study groups designed for teenagers. Two of the highly visible expressions of the current interest in religion are reflected in the attendance at the Mel Gibson motion picture *The Passion of the Christ* and the sales of the books in the *Left Behind* series.

Tens of millions of Americans are turning to what nonbelievers describe as the supernatural in their search for meaning in a culture marked by affluence and anonymity. One example is in the reflections many of the constituents in new missions use to describe themselves and their journey. These reflections cannot be condensed into a short paragraph. For the past quarter century I have been asking the new constituents of relatively new missions a pair of questions. (Full disclosure requires two caveats. First, my sample is *not* a representative cross section of all new missions! It includes very, very few immigrant churches and very few African American missions. It may overrepresent the nondenominational proportion and the missions launched by new denominations that came into existence during the twentieth century. Second, it greatly overrepresents the people who came and stayed. It clearly underrepresents those who came, stayed for several months, became regular participants, but left within a year after their arrival.)

My first question is, "What brought you here the first time?" One group of observations can be summarized by three statements. First, a decreasing proportion are adults born before 1960. Second, rarely do I hear anything resembling, "First of all, denominational loyalty..." Third, I almost never hear any explanation that can be summarized under the umbrella term "geographical proximity."

Many of the responses can be summarized under the label "church shopping." One example, "The church we were in for years called a new pastor we can't stand." Another is, "We moved here from out of town, so we began to shop for a new church home." A third is, "I found myself asking more questions about my own faith journey than the church I was in was answering, so I started looking." Another label for this group is "switchers."

The most common responses, however, can be summarized under the term, "Needs." "We decided we needed a church that was prepared to help us rear our children, and we found it here." "I was a nominal Christian without any church affiliation. I decided I needed a church that would nurture my spiritual journey, and I found it here." "I told a friend at work that I had written off organized religion, and he told me to come and give this church a chance. He came by and picked me up one Sunday morning, and here I found the kind of church I didn't know existed." "One Christmas Eve my husband and I decided we needed to go to church. We looked in the paper and saw this church's ad. We came and we're still here." "My girlfriend insisted I come to this adult Bible study group that was about to be started, and we've never missed a session since. It gave me what I needed, but I didn't know I needed it."

My second question is, "Why did you return and why are you still here?" The responses reflect the big bias in my sample. These responses came almost entirely from the satisfied customers, the happy campers. I do meet the dissatisfied in other congregations, but only rarely are they comfortable describing in detail why they did not return to the first two or three or twelve congregations they visited on their church shopping expedition.

Why did they return week after week? Most of the explanations can be summarized in six words, "My needs are being met here." Other responses resemble these: "This minister is a superb communicator with relevant and inspiring content." "We knew what we wanted, which was a Christian community. We found it here in our Connections Group." "Our teenagers love it here!" In more specific terms, "My spiritual needs are being met here."[5]

The critics describe this as one more expression of how consumerism is dominating the American culture. The professional educators explain, "You can't teach an adult anything that adult doesn't want to learn, so you have to begin with that adult's agenda."

To return to where we started this side trip, contemporary new church development in American Protestantism differs greatly from those two earlier waves. Both of those identified the primary constituents in terms of place of residence, migration, denominational preference, urbanization, age, ancestry, skin color, marital status, and language. That made it relatively easy to design and implement a producer-driven ("This is what they need!") strategy for planting new missions.

Today we live in what is increasingly a consumer-driven ("What are your needs and how can we help meet those needs?") culture. That means using more question marks and fewer exclamation marks at the end of the sentences that are used to direct the design of a strategy. That explains why this chapter concludes with a series of questions. Before looking at those questions, however, we need to take another brief side trip to review two common expressions of interest in planting new missions.

Who Initiates?

"We've been talking about sponsoring a new mission for at least twenty years," observed an influential volunteer at Bethany Church. The occasion was the third meeting of the recently created Futures Committee at Bethany Church, a congregation founded in 1949 as an outreach ministry of

First Church. It now averages nearly 800 at worship, triple the current attendance at Old First Church Downtown. "About a dozen years ago we almost went ahead with sponsoring one, but our associate minister, who was slated to be the mission developer, decided to go back to school, and that was the end of that idea. The possibility has been discussed here at least two or three times since, but nothing was ever done about it. I plan to retire next June, and my wife and I have agreed we would be glad to come on a half-time basis as volunteers for two years to help get a new mission started."

An hour later it was agreed that sponsoring a new mission should be one of the top priorities in the proposed ministry plan for Bethany Church. Six months later that recommendation had become a goal, and a special appeal for designated second-mile contributions to help finance it had raised slightly over $100,000 in cash and pledges. Two of the larger contributions, one from a fifty-eight-year-old widow and one from an early retirement couple, had been accompanied by an offer to match the aforementioned volunteer's commitment of two years of half-time volunteer service.

A month later the governing board at Bethany Church voted unanimously to send a letter to the missions committee of their regional denominational judicatory. The letter stated that in gratitude for First Church's initiative in starting Bethany Church in 1949, Bethany Church was promising a $60,000 grant for each of the first two years plus the half-time services of five volunteers to help plant a new mission on the edge of a large new subdivision being developed on the north side of the city about twelve miles from Bethany's location. Two of those volunteers were core members of Bethany's adult vocal choir, and a third had fourteen years of experience as the volunteer superintendent of the children's division of Bethany's Sunday school. The letter asked the missions committee to make this a priority, to find a pastor who would serve as the mission developer, to prepare a budget for the project, and to provide the balance of the funds required to finance that new mission.

184

The letter caught the members of that mission committee completely by surprise. They had projected plans for five new missions over the next four years, but none of these were on the north side of that city. At that same meeting, the missions committee received a second unanticipated letter. This one came from a family in another part of the state and contained an offer to convey the title to a seven-acre site fronting on a secondary road. The balance of that 120-acre farm had been sold to a residential developer who is planning to construct 300 single-family homes over the next three years. The title to the ten acres directly west of this seven-acre proposed church site already had been conveyed to the local public school district for a new elementary school. The three reservations in the offer were (a) it must be accepted within six months or it will be offered to another denomination, (b) the name of the new congregation must include the words Baxter Memorial Church and (c) the new congregation must be up and running within three years following the date of the transfer of title.

The one member of the missions committee who had received advance notice of this offer stated, "I drove by the property. The proposed church site currently contains the old farmhouse, a barn, and four other buildings. The topography is excellent. Storm water drainage will not be a problem. It is a secondary two-lane country road. The county planning office told me there were no plans to widen it, so the property owners probably will not be asked to donate additional right-of-way in order to develop the land. A realtor estimated the value of that site at $385,000 if developed for residential use. It is currently zoned, used, and taxed as agricultural land. About a mile east of the proposed church site that road intersects with a state road that will become a four-lane divided highway within five or six years. In other words, the proposed site is only 5,000 feet away from being an excellent location. My guess is we could expect, with the right pastoral leadership, that ten or twelve years from now that site could accommodate a congregation averaging 350 to 500 at worship on Sunday morning."

These two case studies taken from real life illustrate four points. First, this is why a separate chapter is devoted to new church development. Second, they illustrate a question about the title to this chapter. Should these three words, "Plant New Missions," be followed by a question mark or an exclamation mark? Third, they illustrate why designing and implementing a turnaround strategy for your denomination may be a far more complicated undertaking than it first appears. Fourth, these two case studies introduce what this traveler has become convinced can be the most productive approach to designing a customized church planning strategy for your denomination. That is to organize the planning in response to a series of questions. Here are a few questions you may want to use in structuring your discussions. This is a much longer list, however, than the five questions on the second page of this chapter!

Twenty-one Questions

1. Who Is in Charge?

Do you design and implement one overall strategy for new church development in all of the United States? If your denomination includes fewer than 1,000 to 1,200 congregations, that might be the most prudent approach. Use a national perspective in defining priorities. Design a multifaceted program for equipping the leadership teams who will plant each new mission.

If your denomination includes somewhere between 1,200 and 4,000 congregations, it probably would be more realistic either to encourage each regional judicatory to design and implement its own strategy for new church development or to design customized strategies for each of four or five regions. If your denomination includes more than 4,000 congregations, it probably is unrealistic to attempt to design and implement a national strategy. One reason is regional differences are too great. Another is the power of regional autonomy. A third is the contemporary role of donor-driven charitable contributions will make it easier to raise money for "our" missional ventures than for national denomination-wide efforts. Overlapping that in several denominations is the current wave of disengagement by congregational leaders from divisive denomination-wide agendas makes it easier to rally support for local initiatives.

That introduces an important facet of this first question that is illustrated by the two case studies. When the focus is on new church development, should your policy-makers react to the initiative of others? Or should they be proactive and design a plan that will guide the decision-making processes? For example, should the people who donate a potential church site control the location and size of that site? Should they also be able to determine the schedule? If they prefer the model that calls for a midsized neighborhood church, should that overrule those who favor planting what are designed to become regional megachurches? Does the donor control the location, design, and timing or does the denomination make those decisions?

To return to the first case study, should your strategy encourage initiative by potential congregations? Should the sponsor choose the location for that new mission? Will those five volunteers select the mission developer pastor they feel will be an ideal team leader? Or should that pastor be free to choose the core volunteer staff? Should that sponsor model that was so effective in 1949 be the model for the twenty-first century? Is $60,000 a year for two years the price tag for control? Should the denominational missions committee be open to initiatives from others? Or should it challenge congregations that have the potential, in terms of discretionary resources, but lack the local initiative to mobilize resources to sponsor specific new missions? Or should the effort focus on mobilizing support for that larger strategy?

A completely different facet of this first question concerns the length of agendas. Do you prefer to add a focus on new church development to an already overloaded national agenda? Or do you prefer to add it to what may be the overloaded agendas of the regional judicatories? Or do you believe it will be easier to administer if new regional agencies are created that include three or more existing midlevel judicatories? Each one would have only one item on its agenda. That would be the planting and nurturing of healthy, vital, and evangelistic new missions. What is your preference? Who makes that decision?

2. What Is the Vacuum?

Does demand create supply? Or does supply create demand? That is a question economists have been debating for generations. When the focus of the discussion is on new church development, the answer may be both or neither.

Back in the post–Civil War era, and again in the post–World War II years, the answer appeared to be both. The organizing of new churches was driven by a demand that had been created by new residential settlements on the western frontier in the nineteenth century and new suburban residential subdivisions in the 1950s. The success of these new missions encouraged others to come in and fill what they perceived to be a vacuum.

The post–World War II era saw few public school districts in the United States offering free kindergarten classes for five-year-olds. The demand by parents born in the 1920s motivated a variety of private organizations, including many churches, to supply half-day weekday classes for five-year-olds. As parents shared their child rearing hopes and experiences with one another, most public school districts began to offer kindergarten classes.

More recently, a growing body of research has documented the value of prekindergarten experiences for four-year-olds and, more recently, for three-year-old children.[6] Once again a variety of private organizations, including thousands of congregations, emerged to fill that vacuum. Demand created supply. As the supply grew, parents began to demand their public schools offer taxpayer-financed prekindergarten classes.

One parallel pattern was the new mission, or the congregation founded decades earlier, that had decided to write the next volume in its history in new facilities on a larger site at a better location, that concluded its primary future constituency would be parents of very young children. A weekday prekindergarten program was organized, staffed, and advertised. Frequently it was publicized under the umbrella statement, "We're here to help you rear your children." A package of ministries was designed that included worship, Sunday school, parenting classes, a ministry of music with children, and vacation church school, with the weekday prekindergaten a prominent component of that package. One consequence was this produced a heavily traveled road for adults who became new members.

Another consequence was an expanded demand for adult learning opportunities.[7] A third was a demand for more ministries with children and youth in first through twelfth grades.

What is the number one vacuum you plan to fill by planting new missions? Is it a vacuum in the ecclesiastical marketplace such as that new residential subdivision designed for 2,500 single family homes? Or a new inner-city church organized around a four-year high school for gifted youth? Or a new mission that will meet in the community center in that new retirement village? Or a new mission led by an immigrant pastor from Mexico designed to serve recent immigrants?

Or is the vacuum in your denominational system in this region? Has the time come to plant new missions to help your denomination reach larger numbers of American residents born after 1960 who trace their ancestry back to

Western Europe? Or is it the vacuum in the predominantly Anglo denomination that is determined to become a multicultural religious body by designing new missions to reach American residents who trace their ancestry back to Africa or Korea or Mexico or Columbia or Haiti or China? Or is the goal to reenter the large central cities in the North such as New York or Detroit or Chicago or St. Louis? Or is the goal to transform what for decades has been a regional denomination into a national church by planting new missions in states in which your denomination has few or no congregations today?

A completely different definition of a vacuum was defined by Sam Walton, the founder of Wal-Mart stores. Walton's first store, which he purchased in 1945, was a Ben Franklin variety store in Newport, Arkansas. Newport was the trading center for cotton and pecan farmers in 1945. Five years later, when the lease expired, Walton's store was the largest Ben Franklin franchise in a region covering six states.[8] Walton, however, decided that Newport, with a population of 5,000, was too large and his store had too much competition for it to become the leader he wanted it to become. He decided the best chances for fulfilling his dream would be to move to a much smaller community with an underserved population and little competition. He chose Bentonville, Arkansas. In 1950 Bentonville had a population of about 2,900 living in 900 houses. This was clearly an underserved country town with little competition.

After prolonged negotiations with the absentee owners, Sam purchased Luther Harrison's variety store in Bentonville and leased the barbershop next door. After remodeling the property, it opened as "Walton's 5¢ and 10¢." Later it was renamed Wal-Mart, and Bentonville became the headquarters for what is the largest retail store company in the world.

The name of that vacuum was "an underserved population with little competition." One version of that on the American religious scene is the small open country Protestant church founded in the nineteenth century that plateaued in size with an average worship attendance in the 50 to 85 range. Three decades ago the minister, after a three- or four-year pastorate, departed for greener pastures. The successor brought an entrepreneurial personality combined with a visionary leadership style. Four years later worship attendance was averaging 160 despite the departure of nearly three dozen members who felt overwhelmed and displaced by that "flood of new people." Today that same minister is the senior pastor of what has become a megachurch averaging over 3,000 at worship. A nearby farm was purchased many years ago to house the physical plant required to serve a constituency living within a thirty-five-mile radius of the meeting place. The post office serving this megachurch is located in a small city seven miles to the south. The majority of the members live in the area to the west. Many reside in a city of 80,000 population or its eastern suburbs. The central business section of that city lies twenty-seven miles west of this megachurch's property.

If your denomination's strategy for new church development is driven by a goal to fill vacuums, should you be looking for places with an underserved population and little competition? Or does some other vacuum drive the design of your strategy?

3. Is Leadership the Key?

For decades the cliché has circulated that the three key variables in evaluting the value of a parcel of real estate are location, location, and location. At least a few experts in new church development have adopted that cliché to declare the key variables in new church development are location, location, and location.

This traveler's experiences suggest that mantra does not reflect the reality of the contemporary world of our church development in Protestant America. If repetition is required, the slogan could be leadership, leadership, and leadership. A variation on that theme could be visionary leadership, entrepreneurial leadership, and long-tenured leadership. A broader definition could be leadership, a precisely defined constituency, and a ministry plan designed to meet the personal and spiritual needs of that constituency. (A surplus of accessible, conveniently located, and safe off-street parking would be one component of that ministry plan.)

If you agree that pastoral leadership is the key variable in determining the success or failure of new missions, that raises two questions. First, do you have an adequate supply of entrepreneurial ministers who bring the gifts, vision, passion, personality, patience, priorities, skills, potential tenure, and experience required to plant new missions?

If the answer is in the affirmative, the next step may be to build a list of those pastors. Identify the next two dozen or two score potential new missions, your judicatory or denomination would like to plant. Prepare a 200- to 300-word description of the primary constituency to be served by each of those proposed new missions as well as the general geographical location. Send to each of those ministers who were identified earlier that collection of possible new missions. The cover letter is a Request For Proposals (RFP), a common practice in the current American economy. Each recipient is invited to submit a detailed proposal for accepting the leadership role in planting that new mission. This would be expected to include a detailed ministry plan, a time line with clearly defined benchmarks for measuring progress, the proposed staff configuration, what this recipient of that RFP would bring in terms of assets (financial support, staff colleagues, volunteers, experience, et al.) and what the judicatory or denomination would be expected to contribute to the planting of that new mission. Each response would be evaluated, and the most promising would move to the top of the action plan.

That door could be opened wider by sending these RFPs to various congregations, the denominational women's organizations, and the denominational men's fellowship in that region as well as to seminary professors and several lay leaders.

If you conclude you have a shortage of ministerial leadership for your needs in new church development, you could expand the circle by circulating the RFP on the Internet, by a national search within your denomination and/or by encouraging several of the larger congregations to fill the position of senior associate pastor with a person who displays the potential to lead a team in planting a new missions but first needs several years of experience in a large church.

If you are convinced a two-week seminar can equip any minister to become the leader required to plant a new mission, you may choose that alternative. If you choose that option, it might be wise to send at least five or six ministers for each slot to be filled. Sort out those "graduates" by asking each one to respond to an RFP.

4. How Do You Define the Primary Constituency?

A large proportion of new missions planted in the United States after World War II was designed "to reach and serve our people who are moving into those new homes." Frequently this included a telephone survey asking the respondents, "If we decide to organize a new church affiliated with thusandso denomination near where you live, would you be interested in helping to start it?"

The primary constituency was identified by place of residence, denominational affiliation, language, skin color, age (most of these new houses were occupied by adults born in the 1910–1930 era), and an interest in helping to pioneer the new rather than joining the old.

In many parts of the nation several denominations cooperated in a comity agreement that also emphasized the importance of geography. A standard rule was a cooperating denomination would not choose a site for a new mission, nor for the relocation of an existing congregation, that was closer than 5,280 feet from the meeting place of a congregation affiliated with a cooperating denomination.[9] That rule enabled noncooperating churches to purchase excellent sites

193

for new missions that were "off limits" for any of the cooperating denominations.

In recent years the new missions that were averaging 500 or more at worship by the end of their fifth year usually can be defined best by the characteristics of the constituency rather than by place of residence or previous church affiliation. From this observer's travels, a dozen of the most common defining characteristics of the constituency of these large and relatively new missions can be ranked in this order.

1. Skin color
2. Language
3. Place of birth
   a. American-born, of grandparents who were born in the U.S.A. before 1920
   b. American-born, of parents who came to this country as adults
   c. American-born, of parents who came to this country as children
   d. Foreign-born adults who came to the U.S.A. as adults
4. Social class and/or upward mobility
5. Self-identified Christians with no active church affiliation searching for a church home
6. Self-identified Christians who were actively involved in a church, became discontented, and searched for a new church. (They left what they had concluded was a "loser" to join a "winner" in the language several have used to explain their switch.)
7. Active church members who moved their place of residence and began to search for a new church home
8. Parents searching for a church to help them rear their children
9. Searchers and seekers who were self-identified nonbelievers on a quest for meaning in life

10. Newlyweds
11. Newcomers to the community looking for a place to meet and make new friends
12. Contented agnostics and atheists who had a life-changing experience that motivated them to begin their own personal search for meaning in life. Positions 4 through 12 on that list vary greatly from one new mission to another.

The reason this question is placed early in this sequence is that it will be easier to design a ministry plan for a new mission, including the appropriate staff configuration, if the constituency to be served is defined early in the process.

A less-structured approach is to choose the general location, pick a mission-developer pastor, and design the ministry plan in response to who shows up to help pioneer it.

An increasingly popular approach begins with the first three of the characteristics (skin color, language, and place of birth) mentioned earlier and followed by a question based on a different perspective.

5. What Stage of the Faith Journey?

Back in the 1950s most new Protestant missions in the United States were launched to reach "the unchurched." There was considerable ambiguity in the definition of that term. Many contended it meant nonbelievers. Others said it referred to Christian believers who were not actively involved in the life of any worshiping community. Frequently the working definition was active church members who had changed their place of residence and were looking for a new church home.

In the 1970s a new term gained popularity. This is the "seeker-sensitive congregation" that focuses on adults who have never accepted Jesus Christ as their personal Lord and Savior, but who are on a self-identified search for meaning in life. Other terms that emerged include searchers, pilgrims, and open-minded skeptics.

195

Concurrently several scholars began to publicize their research that divided the religious pilgrimage of adult Americans into four or five or six or seven stages. The most advanced of these stages was the one that the scholar describing it often revealed was his or her stage.

For this discussion we will divide this pilgrimage into five stages: seeker, believer, self-motivated learner, disciple, and apostle. That matches the number of fingers on my right hand. The seekers, many of whom possess a vague conviction of the existence of a Supreme Being, become open to John 14:6, that the only road to God is through Jesus. Those who accept Jesus as the Christ represent the second stage. Many of them are self-motivated to learn more about the Christian faith. They account for that current huge wave of believers who are engaged in serious and continuing study of the Scriptures. That number in America today is probably twice what it was in 1955 and includes those engaged in a continuing process called "spiritual formation." A much smaller fourth group sometimes describe themselves as "graduates" of that learning stage, which they agree never ends, but are now ready to be challenged and equipped for "doing ministry" under the oversight of those they presume to be at the fifth of these five stages.

While one common assumption is that a new mission should begin by identifying seekers as their primary constituency, this observer has become convinced that an unprecedented large number of Americans today are (a) in that third stage of eager learners and (b) looking for a congregation that will feed their hunger and nurture their spiritual journey. Should those frustrated churchgoers at the third and/or fourth stages be considered as the primary constituency for one of your new missions? Or should every new mission be designed with seekers as the primary constituency?

6. What Is Your Theological Position?

The differences among congregations within a particular denomination are greater today than they were in the 1950s.

That is a product of the rise of individualism, the erosion of vertical lines of authority, ecumenism, the increased level of formal education among adults, the migration of Christians across inherited denominational lines, new sources of immigration, the demands for greater theological pluralism within every Christian religious body in America, and the increased competition among the churches for future constituents.

One consequence is designing a denominational strategy for new church development has become a far more challenging assignment today than it was in 1955 or 1985! That raises three questions worth a brief mention here.

First, do you want all your new missions to be located at the same point on the theological spectrum? Or do you prefer a pluralistic approach with new missions scattered among various points on that theological spectrum? Or do you see this as a minor issue that can be ignored? The answer to those questions should influence the criteria used in choosing mission-developer pastors.

Second, instead of a definition that relies on terms such as fundamentalist, conservative, evangelical, progressive, and liberal, a useful way to distinguish among congregations is by references to the Holy Trinity. If the words used in public prayers, in the text of the hymns chosen for congregational singing, and in the references in sermons are relevant indicators, it is rare to find a congregation that week after week gives equal weight to God, to Jesus, and to the Holy Spirit. In this observer's travels, typically a congregation appears to exalt one person of the Trinity more than the other two.[10]

Which is the dominant pattern in your denomination today? The first-person churches? The second-person congregations? The third-person churches? What do you prefer for your new missions? This also could become a criterion in choosing among candidates for mission developers.

In looking across the broad range of new congregations launched in America since 1985, including denominationally affiliated, independent, predominantly Anglo, immigrant, and ethnic minority, this observer is convinced those now averaging 500 or more at worship come in disproportionately large numbers from among those organized around a focus on either Jesus and/or the Holy Spirit. One *big* exception to that generalization consists of those new missions launched by a predominantly Anglo denomination to reach recent immigrants or American-born blacks that have plateaued in size with an average worship attendance under 100. The usual explanation is they were designed to be small churches. That has turned out to be a more influential than theological stance.

Third, since September 11, 2001, a new emphasis on encouraging interfaith relationships has motivated some denominational leaders to affirm tolerance that can become close to universalism.

Four decades ago the Roman Catholic Church sought to resolve this issue by declaring that the God of Abraham had entered into two covenants—one with Jews and one with those who have accepted Jesus as their Lord and Savior. In recent years more than a few American Protestants have enlarged that concept to include God's covenant with Islam as the third covenant. At least a few others have affirmed a fourth and even a fifth covenant with other religions.[11]

Has your denomination affirmed that special covenant between God and the Jews? Has it also affirmed a special covenant between the God of Abraham and Jesus and Islam? Has your denomination affirmed the existence of a special covenant between the God you worship and other religious bodies? Between the God you worship and secular humanists?

That raises the question of how strongly John 14:6 influences the design of your strategy. That also could become a criterion in selecting mission developers.

7. What Will Be the Central Identity?

What is the central component of the public image or identity of the megachurches of today that were founded before

1995? This observer's travels suggest five common responses to that question. In the smallest number the public image reflects a perception of commitment. "They welcome everyone to come worship, but it's a high threshold into membership! You can't become a member unless you're a tither and a really committed Christian." "That's the easiest church in town to join. Anybody and everybody is welcomed into membership."

The second smallest group enjoys a public image that is a product of a carefully designed, aggressive, persistent, and effective public relations effort. "We do church differently" is one example. "We're a seeker-sensitive church" is another. Third, in a larger number the public image is in the constituency. "That's a Korean congregation." "They have more millionaires than any other church in this city." "That is a cosmopolitan congregation that includes blacks, whites, and immigrants from thirty nations." "That's a gay-lesbian congregation."

A fourth version of the identity is in the ministry. "They have the biggest youth ministry of any church in this county." "That's where single young adults go." "They have the most extensive set of community ministries of any church in the entire metropolitan area." "The waiting list for their Christian day school is three times their enrollment."

Fifth, while this terminology is rarely used, the largest group resembles fan clubs. Instead of being the fan club of a personality in the entertainment world or in professional sports, these are fan clubs of that long-tenured founding pastor or the team leader. "That's Doctor Harrison's church." "Sorry, I can't tell you the denominational affiliation. All I know is Jack Simmons founded it back in 1981, the year after my wife and I moved here."

Do you want to create the dominant public image of your new missions around (1) the level of commitment demanded of those who want to become members, (2) an intentionally designed and aggressively promoted identity, (3) the characteristics of the constituency, (4) the ministry, (5) the personality and public image of the pastor or (6) the denominational affiliation? (That last characteristic did not make the list of the five most common public images.)

8. How Competitive?

When will your denomination encounter the highest level of competition in planting new missions? If the focus is on planting new missions designed to reach people who, except for perhaps being younger, closely resemble the current constituency of your denomination, the most highly competitive areas may be in suburban communities that (a) have been experiencing a rapid increase in the total number of residents and (b) now house three or more Protestant congregations organized since 1970 that average more than 800 at worship.

The American Protestant denomination consisting largely of members who trace their ancestry back to Western Europe also may face substantial competition based on cultural and social class differences—and perhaps on the theological differences—if the focus is on planting new missions in the large central cities designed to reach and serve either recent immigrants or American-born residents who trace their ancestry to Latin America or to Africa or to the Pacific Rim.

Less competition probably will confront the new mission designed to become a large regional congregation or a destination church in rural America. The competition also may be less for the new mission planted in a community that houses a large medical center or a large university or a large theological school that is closely affiliated with your denomination and most or all of the paid staff are affiliated with your denomination.

As you determine the priorities for implementing your church-planting strategy, will the potential competition be a factor in defining those priorities?

9. Do You Affirm Territorial Monopolies?

During the past sixty years an unknown number of proposed new missions have been vetoed by leaders from one or more other congregations who protested to their denominational policy-makers, "You can't do that! To start a new mission so close to our church would be an invasion of our territory." That opposition was justifiable in 1905 but the privately owned motor vehicle plus the rise of individualism has replaced territorial monopolies with competition.

Does your planning for new church development affirm territorial rights? Does it define a congregation's franchise in terms of geography? Does your denominational rule book permit other congregations to compete with your churches? Or does it assume that congregations affiliated with the same denomination do and should compete with one another? Does it assume the privately owned motor vehicle is a passing fad and by 2010 most American Christians will be walking to church?

10. A Great Good Place?

In an exceptionally wise and provocative book, Ray Oldenburg has suggested that most adults in North America and Europe organize their lives around three places. The first place is the home.[12] A good home provides a healthy, supportive, and predictable environment for rearing children. The identity of the adults in the home often can be described by such words as wife, husband, mother, father, disciplinarian, breadwinner, parent, spouse, stepson, in-law, grandmother, or half sister. The second place in the lives of many adults is the place of work. Here one's identity often is described by job titles, expertise, professional competence, the workday, compensation, or duties.

The third place is the focal point of Oldenburg's book. Oldenburg describes the third place as "the core settings of informal public life . . . that host the regular, voluntary, informal, and happily anticipated gatherings of individuals beyond the realm of home and work." The neighborhood tavern is one of Oldenburg's favorite examples of a good third place, but the number of neighborhood taverns has shrunk by at least 60 percent since 1960. That is a reflection of the fact that today's third place rarely can be identified in geographical terms. Fewer and fewer adults "neighbor" with people who reside nearby.

A good third place is where a person is identified by who you are as a person, not by what you do for a living or by your kinship ties. For some farmers in the early years of this century, it was a couple of hours in the blacksmith shop or in the hardware store on Saturday morning. For thousands of today's teenage boys, the gang is their third place. For many choir members, the number one third place in their life is the weeknight choir rehearsal. For others, it may be a bowling league or a service club or a softball team or a bridge club or a book group or a coffee shop or a minor league baseball park.

The crucial distinctive characteristic of a good third place in today's world is that participants eagerly look forward to being with that same group of people in that familiar setting. It is increasingly difficult to identify the participants by the geographical proximity of their places of residence. That group of baseball fans who sit together in the same section of the bleachers may come from a twenty-mile radius.

For the workaholic, the place of work may be today's third place. For hundreds of "snowbirds," the winter residence on the west coast of Florida or in the valley in Arizona or Texas is their third place. For a growing number of Americans born after 1980 their favorite third place is in the virtual world of a computer game.

For millions of long-tenured church members, that congregation is their third place. They eagerly anticipate Sunday morning as a reunion with dear friends they have not seen for several days. This pattern is most clearly visible among some of the older adults in smaller congregations who now live alone and are not employed outside the home. For others, the third place is that adult Sunday school class they helped organize back in the mid-1960s. For many older women, the circle in the women's organization is a favorite third place.

For a few, it is working in the church kitchen. For a growing number, it is that small Bible study or prayer group they helped start several years ago. In a growing number of congregations, the current third places include the mutual support groups created by the leaders of that parish. For some teenagers, with few friends in school, their third place is the youth fellowship.

For millions of Americans in the twenty-first century their favorite third place is a chat room or a mutual support group or a prayer circle on the Internet. For hundreds of young never-married adults, their favorite third place is working with friends on construction of a Habitat for Humanity house. For many it is Wednesday night at church where the schedule begins with a meal and includes a dozen or more groups, classes, meetings, and other gatherings. For a couple of dozen fathers, the new third place is that Saturday morning Bible study and prayer group they launched after attending a Promise Keepers® weekend. The singles group that meets every Friday evening is the third place for many, most of whom are formerly married. For at least a few pastors, their third place is that Tuesday morning with a half dozen other ministers organized around fellowship, coffee, candor, structured Bible study, sermon preparation, mutual support, and unneeded calories.

For some church members, church is strictly a religious place. For others, it is primarily the great good third place in their lives. For many adults, church is a combination of spiritual nurture and a great good place.

Which of your new missions will be designed around worship, learning, and collecting money to hire others to do ministry on behalf of those worshipers? Which will be designed with the added dimension of serving as a great good place?

WARNING! The new mission that begins with two or three dozen people at that first public worship service may evolve into a wonderful third place for most of those charter members. If it does, the next stage may be the transformation of that new mission into an exclusionary fellowship. A more productive strategy is to create six to a dozen third places in that new mission that is averaging at least 300 at worship six months after the first public worship service that was attended by 350 or more.

11. What Else Is on the Agenda?

Three reasons can be cited for the earlier suggestion that new church development be assigned to a single purpose task force or division or committee, rather than to be one component of a larger turnaround strategy, or far worse, one component of a much larger denominational agenda.

The pragmatic reason is the single purpose task force will find it easier to elicit gifts of money and land than will an agenda with several objectives—some of which may evoke negative feelings from potential donors.

A second reason is the value of concentrating time, energy, and attention on one very large and challenging assignment.

The third reason is to avoid diversionary quarrels. If new church development is one item in a ten- or twenty- or thirty-point agenda, it can be challenged by pleas for other priorities. "We need to allocate more money to help our retired ministers!" "Instead of planting new churches, why don't we allocate those resources to revitalizing our aging and numerically shrinking churches." "I believe every new mission should be designed to be a multiethnic and multicultural congregation from day one." (That runs counter to the nature of voluntary associations.) "We need to choose our mission-developer pastors on the basis of ethnicity and gender, not on the basis of gifts, experience, and skills." "Why don't we start more new missions in my state and fewer in your state?" "I believe we should give the money we spend on new church development to the poor rather than on trying to expand our kingdom!"

Fight those diversionary battles in some other forum, not in meetings called to develop a church-planning strategy.

12. What About the Minister's Fan Club?

One of the more divisive issues was mentioned earlier. A disproportionately large number of today's megachurches can be described in these words. "At least two-thirds of the adults are there because they've become members of Pastor Perry's fan club."

Another way to describe that pattern is the contemporary American culture is organized to a reasonable degree around the power of continuing interpersonal relationships. That long list includes doctor-patient, teacher-student, stock broker-investor, auto mechanic-car owner, school bus driver-fifth grader, gang leader-gang member, baseball manager-baseball player, recent immigrant-interpreter, mayor- taxpayer, company commander-enlisted soldier, and pastor-parishioner.

One guiding generalization is the larger the size of the congregation, the longer it takes to include a large number of people in that pastor-parishioner relationship. A second is the larger that pastor's fan club, the greater the shock to the congregational system when that minister departs—and sooner or later all ministers do leave. A third generalization is the greater the degree of the anonymity within a congregation, the larger the proportion of members who place a high value on the perception that "our pastor regards me as a close friend."

From this observer's perspective the two critical trade-offs are (1) the smaller the size of that congregation, the less important is the pastor's fan club; therefore short tenure is acceptable and (2) the larger the size of the congregation, the more valuable as a cohesive force is the pastor's fan club, but that requires a tenure of fifteen to forty years, not five to ten, to maximize that value and offset the downside when the pastor moves.

In designing your new church development, do you prefer larger congregations and long-tenured founding pastors or smaller churches and shorter tenures? Your preference should be one criterion in the selection of mission-developer pastors.

13. Which Immigrants?

A thick book could be written on recent efforts to launch new missions to reach and serve new generations of immigrants to the United States. For this discussion that question is condensed to a half dozen observations.

First, thanks to education, upward mobility, the globalization of the American language and culture, better employment opportunities, and the technological revolution, the Americanization of many of the immigrants from the Pacific Rim has moved at a far faster pace than the Americanization of immigrants from Western Europe in the 1865–1925 era.

Second, one consequence of that is the difficulties encountered in reaching and serving three generations of immigrants from China, Korea, India, Japan, and other nations in the Pacific. Including in one congregation (a) persons who were born in their native land and came to America as adults, (b) adults who are foreign-born and came here as children, and (c) adults born in the United States of foreign-born parents is like pumping water up a steep and high hill. Both skill and persistence are essential.

That immediately raises a significant criterion in selecting a mission-developer pastor. Should that person be someone who came to America as an adult? Or as a child? Or was born in America of foreign-born parents? Or a foreign-born person who is now half of an intercultural marriage?

Third, the Pacific Ocean is wider than the Rio Grande. Designing a new mission for immigrants who plan to return to their native country is a different assignment than designing a new mission for immigrants who came to stay and build their future in America.

Fourth, third-, fourth-, and fifth-generation Caribbean residents with a black skin who come to the United States often do not identify with American-born blacks who trace their ancestry directly back to Africa.

Fifth, long-term financial subsidies to middle and upper class white Americans who are accustomed to subsidies may not be as counterproductive as the promise of long-term financial subsidies to missions designed for recent immigrants.

Sixth, social class distinctions often are highly influential among both white Americans who are the grandchildren or great grandchildren of immigrants from Western Europe and recent immigrants from other parts of this planet.

14. Who Are the Most Neglected?

This month scores of new Protestant congregations will be launched. Many will be designed to reach and serve the new residents of a newly developing residential community. Others will be designed to serve recent immigrants from Nigeria or Mexico or Korea or India or China or Ghana or other countries on this planet. The largest number probably will be designed to reach families with young children at home. Others will be designed to serve residents of a retirement community. A few will be designed to reach single-parent mothers living in low-income housing. Scores will be designed to reach American-born blacks. A modest number will be designed to serve young, childless adults, either married or single.

A relatively small number will be designed to reach and serve a large, rapidly growing, and clearly defined slice of the American population. For comparison purposes, it is useful to note that in 2000, 16.6 million American households consisted of a husband-and-wife couple with one child under eighteen at home. If that category is expanded to include married couples with one or more children under eighteen living at home, the total in 2000 was 24.8 million American households. That is a *big* number and a tempting target population for anyone engaged in new church development.

A sharply different market for church planters consists of people living alone, what the Bureau of the Census describes as one-person households. That number increased from 4 million in 1950 to 11.1 million in 1970 to 27.2 million in 2000 and is expected to reach 34.2 million households by

2010. Approximately one-fourth are never-married adults under 35. At least 15 million have passed their fiftieth birthday. Many of them explain, "We feel like outsiders in the churches that are dominated by younger couples with children, but what else is out there?"

One response to that question is the new mission that has been designed to reach and serve mature adults who live alone. The mission-developer pastor probably will be a mature adult who has been divorced and/or widowed and thus knows what it's like. In addition to worship, learning communities, and opportunities to progress in one's personal faith journey from seeker to believer to eager learner to disciple and perhaps to apostle, the design for this new mission includes a variety of carefully structured opportunities for mature adults to meet and make new friends. These range from eating together to participation in a music group to that ten-day experience as a volunteer short-term missionary to be engaged in doing ministry with fellow Christians in a sister church on another continent to bus trips for a day or two or longer to interesting destinations.

The goal is for this congregation to become the "first place" (see Question 10) in the lives of these mature adults. This worshiping community becomes the place where these folks who live alone feel understood, loved, appreciated, and cared for and enjoy a sense of belonging.

Among the many unanticipated fringe benefits of these ministries with mature adults are (1) marriages, (2) widowed women who replace their deceased husband with a competence, commitment, and love for full-time ministry, (3) volunteers for church-related community ministries, and (4) an unexpectedly early achievement of that goal of financial self-support for that new mission.

A similar model is designed for younger single adults who are interested in marriage but not comfortable in singles bars. Two years after that new mission schedules its first public worship service, the grapevine is carrying the message, "That church is a great place to meet your future spouse." One of the adult Sunday school classes in that second or third program year is designed for newlyweds and engaged couples. The theme is, "How to build a healthy, happy, and enduring marriage." The obvious long-term downside may be that by its seventh birthday, the grapevine is carrying the message, "That's the church for younger married couples."

15. Which Strategy Do You Prefer?

If you decide to give a high priority to expanding your ministry with mature adults in general, and especially that growing number who live alone, how will you do it?

First, you may have to overcome the opposition of those who are greatly concerned about the future of your denomination. "That's a dumb idea! The future of our denomination depends on reaching, attracting, serving, assimilating, nurturing, and challenging the generations born since 1960. Everybody knows that! Let's concentrate all our available resources on reaching the younger generations!"

That argument can generate substantial support. The median age of the American population age 14 and over is between 41 and 42 years. If the median age of your combined membership is in the fifties, those numbers will reinforce the argument.

On the other side of this debate are several considerations that should not be overlooked. First, that high median age among your current members may be a product of the fact that your denomination excels in ministries with people born before 1960, not those born in 1960 and later. Do you want to build your strategy on what you do best? Or on your weakness?

Second, the competition among the churches to reach younger adults is far greater than the competition to reach mature adults.

Third, if the goal is to strengthen the denomination by welcoming more people who will exhibit a strong denominational loyalty, older Americans display a stronger loyalty to institutions than do younger generations.

Fourth, if you place a high value on regular church attendance, on generous financial support of the church and of denominational causes, and on a willingness to shrug off or ignore what others interpret to be divisive issues, American churchgoers in the 60 to 95 age bracket tend to top younger churchgoers on all three of those criteria.

Fifth, if the goal is to make your denomination a stronger institution in 2025 than it is today, what will the churchgoers born after 1960 do during the next two decades? A great many will switch their allegiance to a different religious organization. What will those born in the 1925–1945 era do? Most will die, and many, if encouraged, will remember their congregation and/or their denominational foundation in their wills.

Those are pragmatic, not evangelistic arguments, but they do open the door to a more important question. If you decide to make reaching mature Americans living alone a high priority, you probably will choose from among three different strategies. The obvious one is to plant new missions designed to reach and serve that growing slice of the American population. Some will meet in physical facilities owned by that congregation. Others will worship in community centers and similar settings, but in many other respects resemble a collection of house churches.

A second, less costly, and probably more effective strategy begins by identifying those congregations that currently excel in ministries with mature adults. Your role is to challenge and to help them expand that ministry by raising the quality, expanding the geographical circle they serve, improving and enlarging their efforts to invite mature adults living alone to "Come join us" and to expand their group life, including the creation of what could be described as "our house churches meeting in retirement communities." Instead of being the doer, become the facilitator and a resource.

A third strategy was described in the previous chapter. Encourage the emergence of more multisite congregations.

Challenge some of them to organize new worshiping communities to reach mature adults and/or to adopt and nurture existing small congregations that are doing that and facilitate the expansion of those specialized ministries.

Finally, this policy question should be raised about your overall denominational turnaround strategy. Which components of that strategy should be initiated and implemented by your denominational agencies? Which should be implemented by multisite churches? In looking back from the perspective of 2025, someone may reflect, "One-fourth of what we now describe as new worshiping communities began as new missions planted since 2005, one-fourth were created by our multisite churches and one-half were either relocations of existing churches or the product of congregations that were in existence in 2005 and redefined their role, identity, and priorities, but still gather at that same address."

16. Where Can We Cut Costs?

The one guaranteed outcome in this book is the higher the level of competence and creativity of the people designing a strategy for new church development, the larger the number of meetings of that group and the more frequent those meetings, the greater the probability that the recommendations will exceed the financial resources. One response to that is a brief chapter on paying for this total strategy. Another is to take a quick look at four ways to reduce expenditures.

The three big consumers of dollars usually are real estate, personnel, and inventing how to do church in the twenty-first century.

One alternative on real estate is to meet as a growing collection of house churches and gather for the corporate worship of God on Sunday morning in a community center or public school auditorium or some other rented facility. The cost for Sunday morning use may range from zero to $60,000 or more per year. How much is $60,000? That is the equivalent of 5 percent annual interest on $1.2 million. Why not build or buy a meeting place? One reason is the lack of funds for capital expenditures. A second is, "It's too early in our history for us to know what we'll need ten years from now." A third is owners usually pay for utilities, insurance, maintenance, and custodial service. That rental fee includes those costs.

A variation of this is to rent or lease office space including meeting rooms for seven-day-a-week use and rent that big auditorium with plenty of off-street parking for Sunday morning.

An increasingly common alternative, rather than purchasing expensive land and constructing new facilities, is to purchase or lease "distress" commercial space that may have been designed for a supermarket or discount store and has been vacant for the past year or two. This usually is at a highly visible and accessible location and includes an abundance of off-street parking.

On the personnel question, specialists are replacing generalists. Part-time lay staff are replacing more expensive full-time ordained staff. The bar has been raised on what qualifies as great preaching. Worship teams are replacing full-time ministers of music. Competence is moving ahead of academic credentials in evaluating candidates. The virtual world created by electronic technology has been socializing Americans into a culture filled with projected visual imagery.

One consequence is the campus pastor, assisted by a worship team of lay volunteers led by a part-time specialist, leads the people as they gather for the corporate worship of God. The message, instead of being delivered by a live generalist who earns a grade of B+ on content and B- or C+ on communication skills, is delivered via videotape (or DVD) on a screen by a messenger who is not affiliated with that congregation and who earns an A or A+ on both content and communication skills. That process (a) compensates for the national shortage of ministers who combine the gifts and skills required to be both visionary leaders and superb preachers, (b) solves the problem of "who will preach when our pastor is out-of-town?" (c) eliminates the cost of 15 hours a week devoted to sermon preparation, and (d) leaves a smaller hole when that founding pastor resigns.

The downside, of course, is this is not compatible with the model of building a new mission as the fan club of a magnetic personality who also is a great preacher.

Instead of asking congregations to collect and send money to finance the implementation of a turnaround strategy, a higher priority is given to encouraging qualified congregations to make one or both of two contributions. Those congregations that stand out as successful models of how to do church in the twenty-first century are challenged to accept a role as teaching churches. One models a successful relocation of the meeting place. Another models how to reach and attract families with young children. A third models how to build a staff configuration consisting largely of part-time lay specialists, each of whom is the team leader for a cadre of volunteers. A fourth models the transition from a small rural congregation founded in the nineteenth century into a very large regional church. A fifth models a new mission that averages more than 800 at worship ten years after that first public worship service.

The second potential contribution is to enlarge the number of congregations that have the potential to become large multisite churches. Instead of exporting money, they export "How to do big church in the twenty-first century."

17. Where Do We Begin?

What should be the first priority for the task force assigned the responsibility for church planting?

The obvious answer is to plant new missions! A better beginning point, however, may be to agree on the criteria that will be used in the allocation of scarce resources for new church development. Most of the questions discussed in this chapter were designed to feed the discussion on criteria. Two others, however, should be at or near the top of that list. One was introduced in question 16. Which components of the larger strategy will be implemented by denominational agencies? Which will be implemented largely or entirely by congregations? For example, should this regional judicatory be encouraged to plant a new mission over there? Or should that vacuum be filled by the relocation of an existing congregation? Or should a large multisite church launch a new worshiping community to fill that vacuum?

The second of these two criteria that merit discussion grows out of another question. How do we evoke broad-based support, especially in terms of financial contributions from the laity, for implementing our strategy in church planting?

One answer to that question can be summarized in three words: Success breeds confidence. If the first three new missions to be launched in the implementation of this strategy turn out to be highly successful ventures, it will be easier to raise money for future efforts than if one is a modest success, one turns out to be a good church, and the third disbands after a year or two.

Should pragmatism, as well as ideology, drive the implementation of your strategy?

18. How Many?

How many new missions should you be planting each year? The 1985 answer was, "A number equal to 1 percent of the organized churches in your regional judicatory or denomination every year if the goal is to remain on a plateau in size, 2 percent if the goal is to transform a predominantly Anglo denomination into a multicultural and multiethnic religious body and 3 percent if the goal is to transform a regional religious tradition into a large national denomination." That generalization reflected the American Protestant scene of the 1950 to 1980 era. It also was influenced by the sharp cutback in church planting by several mainline Protestant denominations in the post-1960 era.

How does that guideline fit the twenty-first century? The Baptist General Convention of Texas, a state convention of the Southern Baptist Convention, with approximately 5,000 affiliated congregations, adopted a three-year goal by the Texas Church Multiplication Center in 2001. That goal called for 777 new churches to be launched in the thirty-six months of 2002, 2003, and 2004. The first year produced 264 new missions, and 159 were started in 2003. The starts in 2003 included 75 Hispanic, 32 Anglo, 2 African-American, 20 multiethnic, two Indian congregations, two Vietnamese plus Argentinian, Arab, Brazilian, Guatemalan, Korean, and Laotian starts. That goal of 777 over three years averages out to slightly over 5 percent annually.

That account may be dismissed by those who contend, "But Texas Baptists have a long history of planting new missions. Our denomination hasn't come close to even a 1 percent goal since the 1950s."

Is it possible for a denomination that cut back drastically in new church development during the last third of the twentieth century to reverse that pattern? The Christian Church (Disciples of Christ) with slightly over a half million members in nearly 4,000 congregations in 2000, had cut back to fewer than one half dozen new missions annually during the 1960s.

When Richard L. Hamm was elected to the office of General Minister and President in 1993 and reelected in 1999, he made church planting a high priority. What many, both inside and outside that denomination, regarded as an impossible dream was a goal of 1,000 new congregations by 2020. Thanks to the leadership of the New Church Ministry team, directed by Rick Morse, that impossible dream became a rallying point and evoked a flood of support.

Between the adoption of this goal in 2000 and the end of 2003, a total of 187 new missions were launched with 82 being started in 2003! That undergirded the 2 percent goal with a combination of a challenging vision, a carefully designed plan, aggressive leadership, and confidence that people will respond when confronted with a call to evangelism and mission.

In the American religious environment of the twenty-first century, however, it may be useful to add two other variables to this discussion. One is how do you count the meeting places of that multisite congregation? Do you count it as one? Or six? Or twelve? Or 200? Or do you count the number of new sites added each year, exclusive of adoptions? The other variable leads to another question.

19. What Do You Count?

We count what we believe to be important and whatever we count becomes important. That is a standard guideline in the field of evaluation.

In evaluating a strategy for reaching people with the Gospel of Jesus Christ via new church development, should we count new missions or people? For most of American church history, the focus was on counting congregations. During recent decades the largest 5 percent of congregations account for an increasing proportion of churchgoers. Does that suggest a more useful evaluation process will focus on counting people rather than institutions?

Which represents the most commendable results? Planting three new missions that ten years later report a combined average weekly worship attendance of 4,500? Or planting fifty new missions, of which thirty-five still exist a decade later and report a combined average weekly worship attendance of 3,500?

During the past quarter century, competition has pushed down the cost of groceries, computers, television sets, telephone calls, commercial airline transportation, clothing, and the commission received by stockbrokers. Competition has raised the price of one thirty-second television ad during the Superbowl from $42,000 in 1967 to $450,000 in 1984 to $2.3 million in 2004. Competition also has increased the annual payroll of major league baseball, basketball, and football teams far more rapidly than the increase in the Consumer Price Index.

Competition also has increased the cost of church in American Protestantism. How large must a suburbanite congregation be today to be competitive in attracting and retaining the allegiance of potential future constituents? In most suburban communities the answer is an average worship attendance of at least 450 to 500. In those large suburban communities that report an average annual increase in population of 5 percent or more and that are attracting new missions, the answer is more likely to be an average worship attendance of at least 700 to 800.

The majority of American Protestant congregations average fewer than 80 at worship. Their total annual expenditures usually average out to less than $1,000 times their average worship attendance. For those averaging 100 to 150 at worship, total annual expenditures usually average out to less than $1,200 times their average attendance. For congregations averaging 800 or more at worship, the total annual expenditures are more likely to be somewhere between $1,800 and $3,000 times the average attendance—and $4,000 is not a rare figure! The cost of being competitive keeps climbing in the American religious scene.

If the strategy calls for creating large intergenerational congregations, one component should be a "destination" type congregation averaging 1,500 or more at worship in or near every metropolitan county in the state. Ten of those will include many more people than ten neighborhood congregations resembling the 1955 model that averaged 125 to 160 at weekend worship.

Thus this question of "How big?" should be one variable in that collection of criteria that will guide the design of a church planting strategy. That question also will influence whether an annual goal should be five or ten or two hundred new missions for a regional judicatory or for any one state.

What will you count as you evaluate the year-by-year implementation of your church planting strategy?

20. Soloists or Teams?

Most of the Protestant congregations that have ever existed in America were launched by one person, usually a minister. No one knows whether the definition of "most" is 60 percent or 85 percent or somewhere between, but it clearly is at least 60 percent. The second largest number were "birthed" by a "mother church" that accepted the responsibility for planting new missions.

If you are convinced next year will resemble 1955, those two precedents may guide your planning. Most of your new missions will be launched by a church planter, and the others will be started by a sponsoring congregation.

This observer, however, is convinced that teams are replacing soloists all across the American scene. One example is the team of three to nine people who arrive together to plant a new denominationally affiliated mission. Another example is the self-appointed team of five discontented adults, one staff person, and four volunteers, who leave an established and tradition-driven congregation to go out and launch a new nondenominational worshiping community around the theme of "How to do church in the twenty-first century."

If the design calls for planting relatively small new missions, the soloist often will be able to accomplish that. A reasonable success rate is that five years after the first public worship service, close to one-half of these new missions will be averaging at least 135 at worship and be financially self-supporting in terms of operating costs. Financial subsidies may be needed to help cover capital expenditures, but one purpose of denominations is to redistribute money.

After your task force has reached an acceptable level of agreement on these twenty questions, the time has come to discuss the key variable in determining the success or failure of your church planting strategy.

21. What Is the Road to Success?

Why do so many new missions in American Protestantism either (a) fail to survive to their fifth birthday or (b) plateau in size with an average worship attendance of 125 or fewer? Why do others keep attracting more and more people and eventually grow into megachurches?

While a modest proportion of what turn out to be small churches are the victims of (a) a series of brief pastorates or (b) a severe mismatch between the mission developer and the design or (c) several counterproductive decisions, the vast majority either dissolve or plateau in size because they were designed to be small congregations. One critical component of that design was a staff configuration that was appropriate for a small to midsized congregation.

Why did others grow into megachurches? In the vast majority they were designed to become big congregations and that design included the appropriate staff configuration for becoming a large church. Frequently that meant at least one or two members of the initial staff team brought several years of experience in a very large congregation. They brought some of the insights on how to do big church in the twenty-first century.

A small proportion of those new missions that have grown into megachurches were started by a pastor with a small-church orientation. The design may have called for this to become a big church, but the small-church orientation of that mission developer overpowered the design. After a few years that mission developer was replaced by a successor who either was a self-motivated learner and/or who brought the gifts, skills, vision, personality, theological stance, priorities, passion, and relevant experience required to implement that design.

If your goal includes planting new missions that eventually will average at least 800 at worship, a crucial component of the strategy is to design these new missions to become big congregations. One critical component of that design calls for an attendance of at least 350 at the first public worship service. Do *not* begin by attracting two or three dozen adults who prefer the culture, the intimacy, the simplicity, and the style of a small church! Those are not the people you seek to be the charter members!

Second, begin with the appropriate staff configuration. That means the specialists will outnumber the generalists. That means several members of that team will bring years of experience as members of a very large regional church. That also means the team leader or mission-developer pastor will be of an age to be able to continue as the team leader for at least two decades. That also means the first-time visitor will see and be able to relate to staff "who look like me." That means a passion for ministry will be among the top three characteristics that have qualified that person to be invited to become a member of that staff team. (Some readers will argue that is the number one qualification.)

Third, the temporary meeting place for those first months as a new mission should not impose a low ceiling on how many people can help pioneer this new venture in faith.

Fourth, any promise of financial subsidies for operating expenses should be described in months, not years, and should be accompanied by precisely defined benchmarks for evaluating progress. Do *not* encourage making "renewal of our grant from the denominational treasury" the top concern of the leaders in this new mission.

Finally, that design should place a high priority on taking advantage of the dedication, skills, experiences, wisdom, initiative, and leadership of an ever-growing number of lay volunteers eager to be challenged to be engaged in doing ministry.

CHAPTER SIX

How Do We Pay For It?

While the content and priorities in a turnaround strategy will vary greatly from one denomination to another as well as among the midlevel judicatories in any religious tradition, two components will be present in every one. The first is resistance to the changes required to implement that strategy. A second is implementation will cost money.

That demand for dollars will evoke at least three radically different approaches. The most popular of the three focuses on stewardship. One version of this blames the seminaries for not equipping students to be effective teachers of stewardship when they become parish pastors. A second version focuses on remedial action. This calls for continuing education events to train pastors to be more effective in teaching good stewardship. A third prescription calls for the denominations to produce and distribute the resources required to teach stewardship. A fourth solution is to create a position on the denominational staff for a person who will be responsible for stewardship training. A fifth version of this response calls for training events to help the laity become better stewards of what God has given them.

A second and more pragmatic approach usually is simpler and far more productive. This calls for making approval of the turnaround strategy the one big event at the annual denominational meeting. That is immediately followed by adoption of a plan to launch a two-year capital funds campaign to finance the early stages of implementation. This could include an appeal for designated second-mile giving by individuals, giving circles, congregations, and family foundations. It also could include appeals to individuals or families to contribute the land, or the money to purchase the land, for new missions.

The most sophisticated of these three approaches radically changes the focus of the discussion. Instead of concentrating on stewardship education or fundraising, this approach begins by asking questions. First, what is happening in the American culture in the allocation of those charitable dollars? One answer is that, with an occasional brief interruption, the number of dollars Americans give to charitable causes keeps increasing year after year. A second answer is the competition for charitable dollars is far more intense than it was in 1955 or 1985. Among the most sophisticated and effective competitors are hospitals, museums, institutions of higher education, political campaigns, civic ventures, and a proliferating number and variety of special interest groups and protest movements.

A second question asks, "What is the big change from the donors' perspective?" One is the shift from recipient-driven to donor-driven contributions. Overlapping that is a shift from contributions to institutions to specific and clearly defined attractive causes. A third is that remarkable increase in the number of family foundations. The Foundation Center reported that in 2002 nearly one-third of the dollars distributed to charitable causes by family foundations were allocated to education, one-sixth went to health, one-eighth to arts and culture, one-tenth to human services, one-twelfth to public affairs, and 4 percent to religion. Why was that percentage to religion so low? The most likely explanation is that denominational agencies have not learned how to compete in that arena. How many dollars did your denominational board of home missions receive from family foundations last year?[1]

A fourth change is that to a greater extent than ever before, those charitable dollars travel across a bridge constructed of long-term and continuing relationships between the donor and that persuasive and trustworthy friend who represents that attractive cause.[2] A fifth change is a greater interest by donors in helping to finance creation of the new and a diminishing interest in funding efforts to perpetuate the old. A sixth is churchgoers born after 1960 tend to be found in larger numbers in religious bodies that resemble voluntary organizations and smaller proportions in religious bodies organized on the basis of legal principles. This is an especially significant distinction for the Roman Catholic Church in America and in The United Methodist Church in the United States. A seventh is part of a broader American cultural change. That is the increased demand by donors for transparency and accountability in the expenditure of charitable dollars.

Five Different Appeals

A third question focuses on the differences among different types of appeals for money. From a congregational perspective the first usually is to raise the funds required to finance the operating budget of a congregation. That usually is a relatively easy assignment! Most of those contributions will come from the current incomes of the constituents. A second is the appeal to finance a capital improvements program such as the acquisition of land or the construction of new facilities. The larger the dollar amount of the goal, the more likely that a substantial proportion of the dollars received will come from accumulated wealth.

A third appeal is for money to offset a deficit. One reason this often is a more difficult assignment is it may evoke questions such as "Why do we have a deficit?" or "Is this deficit a product of incompetent management?"

A fourth appeal is for designated second-mile contributions for missions that enable the donor to choose the specific mission to which that donor's dollars will be sent. This often is the easiest money to raise and is used by parachurch organizations as well as congregations and denominations. The higher the quality of the system of accountability, the easier it is to utilize this type of appeal year after year after year.

A fifth appeal in many denominational systems is for a portion of the dollars received by a congregation to be forwarded to help finance denominational budgets. This was relatively easy money to raise back in the 1950s during that peak of denominational loyalty. For several denominations that period extended well into the 1970s. In several cases that loyalty was eroded by a denominational merger. The first big erosion, however, is many members of the generations born after 1940 did not inherit institutional loyalties from their parents. If the American churchgoer born in the 1880–1920 era had survived those born in the 1940–1990 era, this would not be a problem. A more recent trend that has undermined the effectiveness of this appeal can be summarized in seven words: the sharp rise in public intradenominational quarreling. Those public quarrels tend to polarize the constituency, erode denominational loyalty, and reduce financial contributions to headquarters.

One reason for including chapter 2 in this book was an effort to suggest an explanation for why in those denominations in which a growing proportion of the constituents perceive it to be a voluntary association that calls for a different system for raising money. It is increasingly difficult to use that recipient-driven approach in voluntary associations.

In several denominations a frequently heard explanation of the decrease in the proportion of congregational receipts forwarded to regional and national treasuries is competition. Fewer dollars are left to be sent to national denominational headquarters because of the rise in the costs of the fringe benefits, especially health insurance, in the ministerial compensation package; the increased costs to congregations for utilities and insurance; the direct solicitation for members to contribute to church-related colleges, theological schools, parachurch organizations, civic ventures, museums, community ministries, and sister churches on other continents; the increases in the budgets of the regional judicatories; and the recent economic recession.

Another explanation is summarized in the word "disengagement." An increasing proportion of American churchgoers, both Protestant and Roman Catholic, feel disengaged from the agendas and priorities of their denomination. Several readers may contend the appropriate word is not "disengagement," it is "alienation." That introduces the fourth of these five questions.

What Is Counterproductive Behavior?

This fourth question is based on a range of recent experiences. From a financial point of view, what is the most effective way to undermine the implementation of a turnaround strategy? Another way to state the question is how do we minimize our engagement in counterproductive behavior?

One expression of counterproductive behavior is to assume the necessary financial resources can be diverted from the regular streams of income into the denominational treasury. A second is to assume this will be a fully self-financing strategy, and additional funds will not be needed.

A third is to build in generous long-term financial subsidies for perhaps three to five years for several components such as relocations, planting new missions, and the revitalization of dying congregations without building in the necessary criteria for evaluation and accountability. Whether that evaluation of progress is done monthly, quarterly, or semiannually will vary from one project to another. The crucial issue is accountability. That requires precisely stated goals, events, activities, time lines, benchmarks, and agreement on what will be measured and how it will be measured.

A fourth way to undermine the whole effort is to focus the agenda at a denominational meeting on these five items:

1. Approval of the proposed turnaround strategy. This had been introduced earlier so everyone voting will have had at least three months to study it. After a brief discussion, it is approved.
2. Consideration of a controversial and highly divisive report or recommendation. After bitter debate the vote produces a 60-40 division. It does not matter whether that was a majority or a minority voting approval.
3. Consideration of another controversial and divisive issue. After acrimonious debate, it is approved by a 55 to 45 vote.
4. Consideration of a third controversial and divisive issue. After a long, rancorous, and emotional discussion, it is defeated by a 55 to 45 vote. By this time there is a strong possibility that the agenda has been arranged in such a manner that at least two-thirds of the participants will have been on the losing side at least once and another 20 percent will have been on the losing side at least twice.
5. Seek approval of the plan to finance the turnaround strategy.

The agenda resembling this one at a well-attended denominational meeting often produces several predictable consequences. That long list includes (a) increasing the level of alienation among those on the losing side on two out of three of the middle three items on that agenda, (b) reluctant approval of the request for money, (c) among the folks back home, an increase in their level of disengagement, (d) a financial goal for that appeal that is not achieved, (e) an increased willingness among some of the discontented to switch their allegiance to a congregation affiliated with a different denomination or to a nondenominational church, and (f) increased difficulty in raising money in the future for denominational causes.

What Could Be the Most Productive Approach?

We now switch the agenda to a more positive note.

If the polity and culture of your denomination will permit this, the most productive single component in financing your turnaround strategy may be to create a huge number of what are known generically as "giving circles." These usually include seven to fifteen adults who have much in common, such as ideology, priorities in life, age, values, social class, and hobbies. They are relatively homogeneous social networks. A common description by members is, "That group includes most of my closest personal friends." The members of that social network enjoy being with one another. One of the points of cohesion may be travel. Another may be learning. A third may be recreation. A fourth may be entertainment. A fifth may be marital status. A sixth may be promoting a common cause. A seventh may be working together to help those in need. An eighth often is eating together. A ninth may be a hobby.

The two most powerful cohesive forces, however, usually are "we care for one another" and shared experiences. The older the age of the members of that social network, the more likely caring for one another is at or near the top of that list of cohesive forces.

That closely knit social network becomes a giving circle when one member says, "Friends, recently I became interested in a cause (or project or need) that I believe some of you might like to support." That combination of highly valued friendships, trust, and mutual respect for one another makes it easy to win the interest and support of others.[3]

How do you introduce and describe your turnaround strategy to people who could help finance it? At a rally organized around a challenging and inspiring speaker? By

227

distributing printed pieces of paper? By giving each potential contributor a videotape or DVD describing it? By direct mail solicitation? By asking every congregation to fund its fair share of the cost? Via your denominational Web site? By asking congregations to schedule a special offering on a specific weekend? By creating and nurturing prayer circles that will focus their prayers on this venture? By challenging and resourcing every pastor to make this a personal high priority? By diverting funds from other needs to finance this effort? By asking the women's missionary societies to underwrite it? By using income from investments or from your denominational foundation? With the proceeds from the sale of redundant real estate? With very large gifts from a few generous contributors that can be used to challenge people as matching grants? ("For every dollar you give, we have been promised another dollar from this matching grant.") Initially with borrowed money? With money raised from a $100- or $500-per-ticket banquet? By presenting the total strategy as a collection of separate projects, each carrying a price tag and asking individuals and congregations to help fund the one that appeals to them the most?

Most of those alternatives have considerable merit and at least two of them should be included in that five-point plan you are designing to fund your strategy. At the top of that list, however, is the power of friend-to-friend requests for contributions. In the contemporary American culture, in which for many adults personal friendships have moved ahead of ancestry, kinship ties, and religious affiliation in the building of close interpersonal relationships, the friend-to-friend appeal is the most productive way to attract the charitable dollar. This can be an especially productive channel if most of your members were born before 1945 or come from the top two-thirds of the American population in terms of income or accumulated wealth or your constituency includes a substantial number of congregations that average more than 250 at worship (many of these are collections of well-established and tightly knit social networks often identified as vocal choirs or adult Sunday school classes or quilting groups or prayer circles or mission task forces or mutual support groups or learning communities).

In several American religious traditions a different version of these giving circles has been in existence for decades. The chief executive officer of that regional judicatory enlisted several dozen individuals or couples, often to serve three purposes. One was to serve as an unofficial and informal advisory body. The executive would introduce a subject by beginning, "This is what I've been thinking about and praying over. What do you folks think about that?" A second was to serve as an unofficial "voice of the laity." A third was to respond once or twice a year to a plea for financial support of an urgent need. If the next two successors in that office perpetuated that group, it became easy to continue it or to create additional giving circles. Occasionally a critic would describe it as "Doctor So-and-so's personal fan club" or "Bishop Smith's fan club," but it usually produced needed dollars for ministries. That version of the giving circle usually raises somewhere between $200,000 and $2 million annually for that midlevel judicatory. It is a friend-to-friend appeal that will raise far more money in year five of its existence than in year one. It is impossible, however, to reach year five without first passing through years one, two, three, and four. Four dinner meetings a year moves that process faster than only one or two annually.

This concept of friend-to-friend financial appeals built on existing social networks is widely used today to raise money for candidates for election to political office, for colleges and universities, for museums and hospitals, civic ventures, and by a variety of other competitors for the charitable dollar.

The *big* new version of this concept is the virtual community organized around a common cause on the Internet. Howard Dean pioneered that in his political campaign of 2003–2004.

Which of these alternatives are most compatible with the culture, polity, traditions, and values of your denominational system? Don't place all your eggs in one basket! Do not depend on one income stream to finance the implementation of your turnaround strategy! Design and utilize a redundant system that includes at least five different income streams!

CHAPTER SEVEN

THE BIG QUESTION

Has the time come to design and begin to implement a turnaround strategy for your denomination? If you have read this far in this book, your answer probably is in the affirmative. If so, that raises what may be the most controversial and divisive question in the book. Should you design the strategy in-house, by your own staff, and/or by volunteer leaders? Or should you outsource the design to an outside organization that specializes in designing these strategies? Or should you outsource both the design and the implementation of your turnaround strategy?

Before dismissing this as a strange way to end a book designed for denominational policy-makers, please read a few more lines. This is *not* a radical new idea! In recent decades American Protestants have been outsourcing a growing number of needed services and resources. That lengthening list includes specialists to design and staff a capital funds campaign; the demand for new resources for adult Christian education such as the Bethel Series and Alpha; designing, staffing, and administering continuing education experiences for congregational leaders including both pastors and the laity; ministerial placement; sabbaticals for pastors (thanks to the generosity of the Lilly Endowment); equipping adult volunteers as shepherds (the Stephens Ministry); providing a challenging resource for adults eager to live a purpose-driven life (thanks to Rick Warren); sermon illustrations that can be projected on a white screen; resources for Vacation Bible School; inspirational books for Christians seeking to become fully devoted followers of Jesus; a growing variety of resources for youth ministries; consultations with a congregation's Long Range Planning Committee; a denominationally sponsored television series to reinforce the brand name of that denomination; investment counseling services for a denominational pension system; a new hymnal; a new translation of the Holy Bible; a community counseling agency sponsored by several congregations; architectural services; and video games that engage the nine-year-old in the Biblical account of the life and ministry of Jesus.

Individuals and families also are hiring an outsider to do what formerly was the responsibility of a family member. That long list includes changing the oil in the family car; preparing food ready to be served; preparing income tax returns; caring for young children after school; caring for household pets; purchasing and bringing home a week's groceries; the customized tutoring of children; washing the family car; care of the lawn; tutoring teenagers to pass a standardized test; and preparing the body of a deceased member of the family for burial.

Three Basic Generalizations

Outsourcing is becoming an increasing component of the larger American economy. One explanation is the demand for high levels of specialized competence means most organizations cannot provide all the required skills from among the permanent paid staff. A second is outsourcing frequently reduces costs. A third is the larger the size of the organization, the more likely it will specialize in that which it is equipped to do and outsource other needed services. Many public school districts, for example, outsource the programs for special education students and/or the bus transportation required by state law. The United States military forces out-source to civilians tasks once performed by enlisted personnel. Candidates for nomination to the office of President of the United States outsource many tasks, as do candidates for elec-tive offices in state and local government. Hospitals outsource a variety of specialized tasks as, do colleges and universities. The alleviation of world hunger has been outsourced to a variety of nongovernmental agencies (NGOs).

Four Questions

Perhaps the clearest example can be found in choosing a site for a new mission. Should the decision on the location and size of that site be (a) made by a denominational mis-sions committee, (b) outsourced to that loyal family who will donate the land, (c) made by a recently appointed denomi-national official who has had zero experience in new church development, (d) reviewed by that denominational staff member who specializes in risk management, (e) the respon-sibility of a large congregation that agreed to provide the money, staff, and volunteers required to launch that new mis-sion, or (f) outsourced to someone who specializes in site selection for new missions?

Second, if you decide to circulate Requests For Proposals (RFP), should the preliminary draft be prepared by people who have never written such a statement? Or should it be outsourced to an experienced specialist?

Third, should the proposals submitted in response to that request be evaluated by people who have never done that before? Or by experienced specialists?

Fourth, in responding to those and similar issues, what is the value system that drives your decision? A desire to con-tinue to follow procedures and practices inherited from the past? Or a readiness to open the door to a new way to make important policy decisions in a new century?

A preference for the broad-based involvement of "our own people"? Or a willingness to seek experienced expertise on complex concerns?

A conviction that our denomination has its own distinctive culture that makes it impossible for an outsider to be help-ful? Or a recognition that we need all the help we can find as long as the outsider accepts the role of advisor rather than seeks to dominate our policy-making process?

Are we convinced that those who will live with the out-comes of our policies should make those policies? Or do we believe a sound policy will be easier to live with than a coun-terproductive policy?

Do we focus on inputs into our policy-making and since we know more than outsiders about those inputs, we don't need outside specialists? Or do we want to place a high value on outcomes and thus we need help from experienced out-siders in predicting the probable outcomes?

Another Perspective

That annual audit of performance described as possible first and second steps in chapter 1 is a standard operating procedure in profit-driven corporations. It also is an increas-ingly common practice in nonprofit organizations in which the governing board and/or financial supporters and/or clien-tele insist on accountability. It may be the central component of the annual state of the church addressed by a denomina-tional executive. There are occasions, however, where a more detailed evaluation will be required. Planned change may not be possible without a severe shock to what has become a dys-functional system.

What is needed? When? What are relevant diagnostic indi-cators? Here are ten indicators that may be useful in your diagnostic processes.

1. If your denomination or regional judicatory has been experiencing twenty or more years, with per-

haps only one or two brief interruptions, of numerical decline in membership and/or average worship attendance and/or new members received each year and/or baptisms, that may be a signal this religious body no longer is competitive among what is clearly a growing number of Protestant churchgoers in America.

2. If the median age of the current membership, age 14 and over, is older than age 50, that suggests an erosion of the capability to reach and serve younger generations or recent immigrants. (In 2005, the median age of the American population, age 14 and over, was slightly under 42 years.)

3. If the total number of new missions started during the last five years averages out to fewer per year than the equivalent of one-half of 1 percent of the current number of organized churches, that suggests an operational policy has been accepted to become older and smaller.

4. If more than one-half of the new missions launched during the past ten years (a) do not average at least 135 at worship or (b) no longer exist, that suggests the time has come to review the policies and practices guiding that part of your denominational agenda.

5. If fewer than 5 percent of all organized churches averaged more than 500 at worship last year, that suggests one of four possibilities: (a) the long-term denominational strategy is focused on building the future in nonmetropolitan America, (b) that long-term strategy is driven by a conviction that the future of American Protestantism is with small and midsized congregations, (c) the evangelistic outreach is focused on people born before 1960, or (d) a preference for short pastorates drives the ministerial placement system.

6. If the population of the territory served by your denomination, or regional judicatory, has increased by at least 10 percent since 1960 and if the number of congregations affiliated with your denomination in that territory has decreased by more than 10 percent since 1960, that suggests you are faced with either a problem or a crisis, depending on the size of the gap between those two trend lines.

7. If there is an absence of broad-based agreement on whether this denomination is located near the end of the institutional spectrum, described in chapter 2 as a voluntary association, or toward the other end, described as a covenant community based on clearly defined and widely affirmed legal principles, this suggests the door has been opened to diversionary intradenominational quarreling.

8. If there is common agreement that "the disengagement of a growing proportion of the laity from our denominational agenda is one of our problems," that suggests that lay support for a turnaround strategy may evoke more yawns than actual support.

9. If several of the most well-informed volunteer leaders are convinced "Our basic problem is the denial that we have a problem," that suggests the time has come to flood the system with relevant information.

10. If there is widespread agreement among the most influential full-time paid staff that, "The time has come to redesign our organizational structure, but we can do that without any outside help," that may suggest an outside perspective could be helpful.

If your response to seven of those ten indicators is, "That describes our situation," you may be well-advised to call for a more comprehensive analysis of your denominational system. Three recent and widely publicized examples of the value of turning to a special commission that includes outsiders with specialized and relevant capabilities revealed four common threads.[1] First, it is reasonable to expect the insiders of any bureaucratic system will defend that institution and its past actions. Second, it is unreasonable to expect those same insiders to be able and willing to conduct a comprehensive and critical analysis of any systems failure in that institution.

Third, rarely is it possible to "fix the current system" without challenging and changing the institutional culture.[2] For example, a common characteristic of a failing institutional culture is that entitlements, based on precedents from the past, create a barrier to fufilling demands for accountability based on actual outcomes compared to desired outcomes. That focus on inputs into each component of the larger system may mean tradition has replaced purpose in the allocation of scarce resources.

Fourth, when the final prescription is condensed into "change, or become obsolete," the response often focuses on "why we cannot make those changes."

When those patterns are translated into how a mainline denomination in contemporary American Protestantism can design and implement a customized turnaround strategy, five probable outcomes float to the surface and rank from easy to exceptionally difficult.

The easiest one to achieve is to resist all changes that threaten the current corporate culture and continue on that downward curve.

The second easiest to implement is to move the institution into a state of denial.

The third easiest is to open that safety valve called "withdrawal" and encourage, or at least permit, discontented individual church members, clergypersons, and congregations to withdraw and transfer their allegiance to other religious bodies.

The fourth easiest, or the second most difficult road to take, is a reasonably peaceful schism.

The most difficult requires distinguishing between symptoms (the first six of those ten diagnostic patterns described earlier) and systemic failures. The temptation is to attempt to fix what has become a dysfunctional system. This most difficult assignment requires digging beneath those undesired outcomes and focusing on the systemic changes required for that organization to be able to produce the desired outcomes. One barrier is an absence of agreement on those desired outcomes.

A useful response can be to appoint and staff an independent commission that will analyze the historical record, the institutional culture, and the organizational structure. That commission also should recommend the changes required to enable the denomination to fulfill its original purpose in evangelism and missions and in resourcing congregations. That is an unrealistic assignment for insiders to fulfill if they are driven by attachment to the status quo or by a desire to justify their own earlier decisions and actions!

NOTES

Introduction

1. The ten contemporary successors to those three dozen denominations referred to here are the American Baptist Churches in the U.S.A., the Christian Church (Disciples of Christ), the Episcopal Church USA, the Evangelical Lutheran Church in America, the Lutheran Church-Missouri Synod, the Presbyterian Church (USA), the Reformed Church in America, the United Church of Christ, The United Methodist Church, and the Wisconsin Evangelical Lutheran Synod.

1. What Happened?

1. This brief account is based on Matthys Levy and Mario Salvadori, *Why Buildings Fall Down* (New York: W. W. Norton, 2002), pp. 221-30.

2. For a more extended discussion of the changes in the world of American philanthropy, see Lyle E. Schaller, *The New Context for Ministry: Competing for the Charitable Dollar* (Nashville: Abingdon Press, 2002), pp. 105-333.

3. Lyle E. Schaller, *Community Organization: Conflict and Reconciliation* (Nashville: Abingdon Press, 1966).

4. Rob Weber, *Visual Leadership: The Church Leader as ImageSmith* (Nashville: Abingdon Press, 2002).

5. An excellent introduction to Deming's work is Mary Walton, *The Deming Management Method* (New York: Putnam, 1986).

6. An earlier effort by this observer was Lyle E. Schaller, *Discontinuity & Hope* (Nashville: Abingdon Press, 1999).

7. Robert William Fogel, *The Fourth Great Awakening & the Future of Egalitarianism* (Chicago: University of Chicago Press, 2000).

8. See D. G. Hart, *That Old-Time Religion in Modern America* (New York: Ivan R. Dee, 2002); Christian Smith, *American Evangelicalism: Embattled and Thriving* (Chicago: University of Chicago Press, 1998); Alan Wolfe, *The Transformation of American Religion* (New York: Free Press, 2003). These three books provide excellent descriptions of recent

changes in American Protestantism. A shorter summary is Richard Wightman Fox, "America's National Obsession," *The Chronicle of Higher Education* (February 20, 2004): B7-10. Rather than rely on such categories as "liberal" or "conservative" or "progressive" or "evangelical" or "fundamentalist" or "enlightened" in describing this doctrinal chasm in contemporary American Protestantism, it may be more useful to use that distinction between Jerusalem and Athens described by James Nuechterlein, "Athens and Jerusalem in Indiana," *The American Scholar* (Summer 1988): 353-68.

9. One example of liberal-conservative Protestant coalitions opposed to Roman Catholicism is described in Robert Moats Miller, *Bishop G. Bromley Oxnam: Paladin of Liberal Protestantism* (Nashville: Abingdon Press, 1990), pp. 398-446.

10. An interesting interpretation of one of these is Margaret M. Poloma, *The Assemblies of God at the Crossroads* (Knoxville: University of Tennessee Press, 1989).

11. A review of Gibson's movie that focuses on the symbolism of the cross is John A. Coleman, SJ, "Mel Gibson Meets Marc Chagall," *Commonweal* (February 27, 2004): 12-15.

12. This distinction among Protestant congregations is described in greater detail in Lyle E. Schaller, *Looking in the Mirror* (Nashville: Abingdon Press, 1984), pp. 73-88.

13. An excellent collection of reflections on a pioneering Protestant merger three decades later is Dorothy C. Bass and Kenneth B. Smith, eds., *The United Church of Christ: Studies in Identity and Polity* (Chicago: Exploration Press, 1987).

14. B. Joseph Pine II and James H. Gilmore, *The Experience Economy* (Boston: Harvard University Business School Press, 1999).

15. This and related issues are discussed in Lyle E. Schaller, *44 Questions for Church Planters* (Nashville: Abingdon Press, 1991).

16. Lyle E. Schaller, *Small Congregation, Big Potential* (Nashville: Abingdon Press, 2004), pp. 79-103.

17. An excellent introduction to this subject is Aaron Wildavsky, *The Rise of Radical Egalitarianism* (Washington, D.C.: American University Press, 1991). Another provocative analysis is Herbert J. Gans, *Middle American Individualism* (New York: Oxford University Press, 1991). An earlier and highly influential book was William Glasser, *The Identity Society* (New York: Harper & Row, 1972).

18. An exceptionally comprehensive and highly provocative research report on disengagement is William Sachs and Thomas Holland, *Restoring the Ties That Bind* (New York: Church Publishing, 2003). The authors point out that the disconnection between the horizontal partnerships in parishes and the vertical structure of the Episcopal Church is at the heart of the contemporary crisis in that denomination. This is the only book

referred to in this volume that should be considered as "must read" by anyone involved in designing new denominational systems.

19. For an historical treatment of this subject see Robert H. Wiebe, *Self-Rule: A Cultural History of American Democracy* (Chicago: University of Chicago Press, 1995).

20. In a fascinating book one scholar has pointed out that during the second quarter of the nineteenth century evangelical Protestantism was a powerful bond of national unity in the United States. When the Methodists, the Baptists, and the Presbyterians split, that suggested that if good Christians could not reconcile their differences and continue together, it was inevitable that slavery would divide the nation. C. C. Goen, *Broken Churches, Broken Nation* (Macon, Ga.: Mercer University Press, 1985).

21. This concept of nongeographical affinity judicatories is described in broader terms in Lyle E. Schaller, *From Geography to Affinity* (Nashville: Abingdon Press, 2003).

22. These and other alternatives are discussed at greater length in Lyle E. Schaller, *What Have We Learned?* (Nashville: Abingdon Press, 2001), pp. 197-213.

23. A superb discussion of the consequences of the decline in civility is Stephen Carter, *Civility* (New York: HarperCollins, 1998).

24. Will Herberg, *Protestant, Catholic, Jew* (New York: Doubleday & Company, Inc., 1956). Nearly forty years after the publication of Herberg's classic, it was reviewed by Joel Schwartz in *The Public Interest*, a quarterly devoted to public affairs in America. That entire issue for Spring 2004 focused on "Religion in America." In his review Schwartz agrees with Herberg that Americans were and are both religious and secular, but he lifts up several changes in the American religious scene since Herberg wrote. One is a sharp increase in marriage across religious lines. A second is that the internal harmony within most religious bodies of the 1950s has been replaced by discord and controversy. A third change is Herberg dismissed the religious bodies outside mainline American Protestantism as having a limited future. Instead they have grown while the mainline denominations have shrunk in numbers.

25. The pioneering book on the emergence of entertainment as a central theme in the American culture is Neil Postman, *Amusing Ourselves to Death* (New York: Penguin Books, 1985).

26. Andrew J. Polsky, *The Rise of the Therapeutic State* (Princeton, N.J.: Princeton University Press, 1991).

27. Marsha G. Witten, *All Is Forgiven: The Secular Message in American Protestantism* (Princeton, N.J.: Princeton University Press, 1993). Witten found both Presbyterian and Southern Baptist preachers were delivering the message that portrayed God as a "loving and understandable Daddy." Another professor, Lori Carrell, *The Great American Sermon Survey* (Wheaton, Ill.: Mainstay Church Resources, 2000), insists

preaching should and can be two-way communication that speaks to the agendas brought by worshipers.

28. Robert D. Putnam, *Bowling Alone* (New York: Simon & Schuster, 2000) and Robert D. Putnam and Lewis M. Feldstein, *Better Together* (New York: Simon & Schuster, 2003).

29. Paul K. Conklin, *The Uneasy Center* (Chapel Hill: University of North Carolina Press, 1995).

30. Roger Finke and Rodney Stark, *The Churching of America 1776–1990: Winners and Losers in Our Religious Economy* (New Brunswick, N.J.: Rutgers University Press, 1992).

31. Bureau of the Census, Department of Commerce and Labor, *Religious Bodies: 1906* (Washington: Government Printing Office, 1910).

32. The primary source for the membership data for 1953 was Frank S. Mead, *Handbook of Denominations in the United States* (Nashville: Abingdon Press, 1956), pp. 217-24. Denominational reports were used for calculating the ratios for 2000 when the population of the United States was reported to be 286 million.

2. Which Rule Book?

1. The contents of this chapter can be traced back to my study of comparative government in graduate school at the University of Wisconsin, nearly seven years work in municipal government, and five decades of working with nonprofit institutions. The most useful single book has been *Voluntary Associations*, edited by J. Roland Pennock and John W. Chapman (New York: Atherton Press, 1969). When the focus is narrowed to high commitment organizations, research on military organizations naturally become a rich resource since the highest commitment is a willingness to die for a cause or a crusade. Recent essays on suicide bombers lift up the power of religion. One classic book grew out of the conflict in Vietnam, Richard A. Gabriel, *Crisis in Command* (New York: Hill and Wang, 1978). It explains many of the factors behind the crises faced by several mainline Protestant denominations as well as the current crisis in the Roman Catholic Church in America. For those interested in how to build a high commitment covenant community, Thomas E. Ricks, *Making the Corps* (New York: Scribner, 1997) contains dozens of lessons that can be translated into relevant concepts for building a high commitment religious community.

2. An excellent reference for the discussion over nullification is *John C. Calhoun*, edited by Margaret L. Coit (Eaglewood Cliffs, N.J.: Prentice-Hall, 1970). Professor Coit had earned a Pulitzer Prize in 1950 for her biography of John C. Calhoun. Twenty years later, in this series, *Great Lives Observed*, she has brought together relevant writings by Calhoun, commentaries on his political philosophy by Calhoun's contemporaries, as

well as subsequent evaluations by historians. The Ordinance of Nullification is reprinted as item 143 in *Documents of American History*, 3rd ed., edited by Henry Steele Commanger (New York: F. S. Crofts & Co., 1946), pp. 261-62.

3. A superb analysis of that 1960s demand for participatory democracy is Daniel P. Moynihan, *Maximum Feasible Misunderstanding* (New York: Free Press, 1969). This observer's reflections on that subject can be found in Lyle E. Schaller, *Community Organization: Conflict and Reconciliation* (Nashville: Abingdon Press, 1966) and *The Churches' War on Poverty* (Nashville: Abingdon Press, 1967), pp. 94-128.

4. Frederick V. Mills, Sr., *Bishops By Ballot* (New York: Oxford University Press, 1978), pp. 288-307.

5. Lyle E. Schaller, *The New Context for Ministry: Competing for the Charitable Dollar* (Nashville: Abingdon Press, 2002), pp. 273-312.

6. This right of nullification in both doctrine and polity was demanded repeatedly by the clergy in The United Methodist Church during the early years of the twenty-first century and has become a polarizing issue within that denomination.

7. This is a major theme of William Sachs and Thomas Holland, *Restoring the Ties That Bind* (New York: Church Publishing Incorporated, 2003).

8. One model of how to organize a regional judicatory around missions and evangelism is described in Claude E. Payne and Hamilton Beazley, *Reclaiming the Great Commission* (San Francisco: Jossey-Bass, 2000).

9. Dorothy C. Bass and Kenneth B. Smith, eds., *The United Church of Christ: Studies in Identity and Polity* (Chicago: Exploration Press, 1987).

3. Designing a Turnaround Strategy

1. This line of demarcation between Jerusalem and Athens has been described by James Nuechterlein, "Athens and Jerusalem in Indiana," *The American Scholar* (Summer 1988): 353-68.

2. For suggestions on the role and identity of these congregations see Lyle E. Schaller, *The Very Large Church* (Nashville: Abingdon Press, 2000).

3. J. William Youngs, Jr., *God's Messengers: Religious Leadership in Colonist New England, 1700–1750* (Baltimore: Johns Hopkins University Press, 1976), p. 143.

4. For an explanation for the diminishing number of American Protestant pastors who stand in one place for twenty or more minutes while reading a sermon out loud, see Nick Morgan, "The Kinesthetic Speaker: Putting Actions into Words," *Harvard Business Review* (April 2001): 113-20.

5. One useful recent commentary on religion in contemporary America is Alan Wolfe, *The Transformation of American Religion* (New York: Free Press, 2003). Another is the collection of essays in *The Public Interest* (Spring 2004).

6. Lyle E. Schaller, *From Geography to Affinity: How Congregations Can Learn From One Another* (Nashville: Abingdon Press, 2003).

7. Lyle E. Schaller, *The Evolution of the American Public High School* (Nashville: Abingdon Press, 2000).

8. Essential reading for anyone responsible for learning communities for Americans born after 1985 is James Paul Gee, *What Video Games Have to Teach Us about Learning and Literacy* (New York: Palgrave/St. Martin's Press, 2003).

9. B. Joseph Pine II and James H. Gilmore, *The Experience Economy: Work Is Theatre and Every Business a Stage* (Boston: Havard Business School Press, 1999).

10. Jim Collins, *Good to Great* (New York: Harper Business, 2001).

11. The Key Church Strategy is described in J V Thomas and J. Timothy Ahlen, eds., *One Church, Many Congregations* (Nashville: Abingdon Press, 1999).

12. My first book, *Planning for Protestantism in Urban America*, was published by Abingdon Press in 1965. I gave copies to several friends including a couple of black pastors. One chapter focused on successful efforts by previously all-white congregations to reach, attract, and assimilate American-born blacks. Several months later a close personal friend, who was the pastor of a large Christian Methodist Episcopal Church, asked me if I knew what I was trying to do with that chapter. I explained in a positive and optimistic statement that my goal was to encourage the racial integration of the churches. In a gentle and nonthreatening manner, my friend corrected me. "No, Lyle, what you are encouraging is the undermining of the strongest institution in the Negro community." That day I began to realize there may be two sides to nearly every issue.

13. Thirty-nine years later I described a possible scenario in which white congregations could unite with a predominantly black denomination. Lyle E. Schaller, *The Ice Cube Is Melting* (Nashville: Abingdon Press, 2004), pp. 183-85.

14. This distinction is described in Lyle E. Schaller, *What Have We Learned?* (Nashville: Abingdon Press, 2001), pp. 197-213.

15. Options for staffing small churches are discussed in Lyle E. Schaller, *Small Congregation, Big Potential* (Nashville: Abingdon Press, 2003), pp. 71-103.

4. The Multisite Option

1. A brief introduction to the multisite concept can be found in Lyle E. Schaller, *Innovations in Ministry* (Nashville: Abingdon Press, 1994), pp. 86-133.

2. The Key Church Strategy is described in J V Thomas and J. Timothy Ahlen, *One Church, Many Congregations* (Nashville: Abingdon Press, 1999).

3. The normative size of congregations in American Protestantism is discussed in Lyle E. Schaller, *Small Congregation, Big Potential* (Nashville: Abingdon Press, 2003), pp. 23-26, 39-54, 205-9.

4. The adoption model is described in more detail in Schaller, *Small Congregation, Big Potential*, pp. 79-92.

5. Quoted in Joe Feuerherd, "Priestless Sundays a Contentious Issue," *National Catholic Reporter* (November 21, 2003): 5.

6. The affiliate relationship is described in Schaller, *Small Congregation, Big Potential*, pp. 93-103.

5. Plant New Missions

1. These data are from *Religious Bodies: 1906*, Part I, a report on the special census of religious bodies in the United States carried out by the United States Bureau of the Census and published in 1910 (Washington: Government Printing Office).

2. The primary source for these statistics is Louis W. Bloede, "Development of New Congregations in the United States and Canada by the Evangelical United Brethren Church," an unpublished Doctor of Theology dissertation for the School of Theology, Boston University, 1960. In addition, Bloede has accumulated similar data on new church development from a half dozen denominations plus visits to over 200 independent churches.

3. Robert William Fogel, *The Fourth Great Awakening & the Future of Egalitarianism* (Chicago: University of Chicago Press, 2000).

4. One example is the section on "Things Go Better With God," *The American Enterprise* (October/November 2003): 4-8.

5. This is a central theme of a major research project reported in William Sachs and Thomas Holland, *Restoring the Ties That Bind* (New York: Church Publishing, Incorporated, 2003).

6. There is a wealth of research documenting the value of early childhood development programs. Susan B. Neuman, "From Rhetoric to Reality: The Case for High-Quality Compensatory Prekindergarten Programs," *Phi Delta Kappan* (December 2003): 286-91, summarizes recent research. A historical review is Ann Hulbert, *Raising America: Experts, Parents and a Century of Advice about Children* (New York: Knopf, 2003). A summary of three studies is Gerald W. Bracey and Arthur Stellar, "Long-Term Studies of Preschool: Lasting Benefits Far Outweigh Costs," *Phi Delta Kappan* (June 2003): 780-83.

7. An exceptionally valuable resource for anyone teaching teenagers or adults is Ken Bain, *What the Best College Teachers Do* (Cambridge, Mass.: Harvard University Press, 2004).

8. Bob Ortega, *In Sam We Trust* (New York: Times Business, 1998), pp. 25-40. A parallel account can be found in Sandra S. Vance and Roy V.

Scott, *Wal-Mart* (New York: Twayne Publishers, 1994), pp. 8-100. An autobiographical account of Sam Walton with John Huey is *Sam Walton: Made In America* (New York: Doubleday, 1992), pp. 21-31.

9. Comity flourished back in an era when the perception of a scarcity of resources encouraged interdenominational cooperation. The increase in the level of competition among the churches for future constituents was among the forces that brought an end to comity. See Lyle E. Schaller, *Planning for Protestantism in Urban America* (Nashville: Abingdon, 1965), pp. 85-112.

10. This distinction is discussed in greater detail in Lyle E. Schaller, *Looking in the Mirror* (Nashville: Abingdon Press, 1984), pp. 74-88.

11. A challenging and open-minded discussion of whether a monotheist can accuse another monotheist of worshiping a different God is offered by Jon D. Levenson, "Do Christians and Muslims Worship the Same God?" *Christian Century* (April 20, 2004): 32-33.

12. Ray Oldenburg, *The Great Good Place* (New York: Paragon House, 1989).

6. How Do We Pay For It?

1. An excellent historical review of the emergence of foundations in American philanthropy is Eleanor L. Brilliant, *Private Charity and Public Inquiry* (Bloomington, Ind.: Indiana University Press, 2000).

2. For a more extensive discussion of raising money for denominational causes see Lyle E. Schaller, *The New Context for Ministry* (Nashville: Abingdon Press, 2002), pp. 273-312.

3. For a more detailed discussion of giving circles see Suzanne McGee, "Charity in the Round," *Robb Report Worth* (March 2004): 118-20.

7. The Big Question

1. For an excellent summary of the investigation of the destruction of the *Columbia* space vehicle and a provocative introduction to the concept of an outside audit of the performance of a large institution, see William Langewiesche, "Columbia's Last Flight," *The Atlantic Monthly* (November 2003): 56-87. The account by a former insider of a great American institution on the brink of a crisis is Howell Raines, "My Times," *The Atlantic Monthly* (May 2004): 49-81. The report of the bipartisan commission to investigate the events leading up to the terrorist attack of September 11, 2001 received wide national publicity in the summer of 2004.

2. One of the earliest contributions to the power of institutional cultures that has stood the test of time is Terrence E. Deal and Allen A. Kennedy, *Corporate Cultures* (Reading, Mass.: Addison-Wesley Pub., 1982).